MW00878474

THE 100 GREATEST OF MILITARIES THROUGHOUT HISTORY

Table of Contents

Introduction 1

    The Significance of Military History 3

Ancient Era 5

    Overview of Influential Ancient Military Forces..................... 5

        Roman Empire (c. 27 BC-476 AD)... 5

        Persian Empire (550 BC-330 BC) 6

        Ancient Chinese Armies (c.1122 BC-221 BC)....................... 6

    Key Strategies, Technologies, And Battles.............................. 7

    Relationship Between Political Powers and Military Might...... 9

Ancient Near East and Far East Militaries 12

    Exploration Of Military Powers... 12

        Babylonians: The Rulers of Mesopotamia........................... 12

        Assyrians: Masters of War... 12

        Hittites: The Iron Warriors 13

    Early Chinese Dynastic Armies and Their Warfare Tactics 14

    The Rise of The Ancient Japanese Samurai Class 16

Medieval and Renaissance Militaries.....................................19

    Military Powers of the Middle Ages and Renaissance Period. 19

    Highlighting Advancements in Weaponry, Tactics, and Conquests 21

    Importance Of Religion and Chivalry in Shaping Medieval Warfare... 23

Early Modern Period Militaries in Europe 25

    Examination Of Military Developments During The 18th Century... 25

Industrial Revolution and its Impact............................... 27

The Infamous Pirate Age and Privateering............................ 29

Early Modern Period Militaries in Asia and Africa 32

Overview of Influential Militaristic States........................ 32

Military Technologies and Strategic Innovations 34

Influence of European Powers on Shaping their Military........ 36

Latin American Revolutionary Wars & Independence Movements..39

Examination of Key Military Forces............................... 39

Emphasis on Prominent Leaders.................................... 41

Analysis of Guerilla Tactics in Latin American Conflicts....... 43

19th Century Imperialism & Colonization..........................46

The Role of Major Imperial Powers' Militaries 46

Colonial Wars and Resistance Movements........................... 48

Impact On Global Military Landscape............................... 50

Militaries in the Age of World War I 53

Analysis of Influential Militaries in World War I................. 53

Entente Powers 53

Central Powers 54

Trench Warfare Tactics and Technological Advancements 55

Social, Economic, and Political Effects 57

Social Effects... 57

Economic Effects 58

Political Effects 59

Militaries in the Age of World War II **60**

Assessment of Influential Militaries in World War II 60

The Allies: United States, Soviet Union, and Great Britain . 60

The Axis Powers: Germany, Italy, and Japan..................... 61

Notable Militaries: Finland, China, and France 61

Technological Advancements, Warfare Strategies, and Global Impact... 62

Exploration of the Holocaust and War Crimes 64

Cold War Militaries...**67**

Review Of Superpower Militaries: United States Vs. Soviet Union... 67

Key Proxy Conflicts and Related Military Forces 69

The Nuclear Arms Race and Mutually Assured Destruction... 71

Modern Era and Contemporary Militaries...........................**74**

Discussion Of Current Military Powers................................. 74

Emphasis On Modern Warfare, Cyber Capabilities, And Geopolitical Influence... 76

Modern Era and Contemporary Military Challenges.............. 78

Beyond Borders: Unconventional Militaries and Insurgent Forces **81**

Exploration of Non-State Actors, Insurgent Groups, and Unconventional Warfare Tactics... 81

Case Studies on Guerrilla Warfare, Terrorism, And Cyber Threats.. 83

Guerrilla Warfare: The Vietnam War 83

Terrorism: The September 11 Attacks 84

Cyber Threats: The Stuxnet Worm.................................. 84

Examination of Paramilitary Forces and Their Influence on Armed Conflicts 85

Military Innovations and Future Trends.....................................88

Cutting-Edge Military Technologies and Innovations............. 88

    Drones: Revolutionizing Aerial Warfare.............................. 88

    Space Warfare: The Next Frontier....................................... 88

    Hypersonic Weapons: A New Generation of Speed and Lethality.. 89

    Advanced Armor and Exoskeletons 90

Speculation on Future Trends and Potential Shifts in Global Military Dominance 90

Ethical Considerations for Future Warfare Technologies........ 93

Conclusion 96

Reflection On the Evolution of Warfare and Its Impact on History and Geopolitics 97

APPENDIX...99

Additional Information on Military Leaders, Influential Battles, and Further Reading Suggestions 99

    Military Leaders... 99

    Influential Battles 99

    Further Reading Suggestions.. 100

Glossary of Terms and Concepts 101

Introduction

The *"100 Greatest of Militaries Throughout History"* aims to provide readers with a comprehensive understanding of the most remarkable military forces that have shaped human civilization. In order to develop a list that genuinely reflects the magnitude of these militaries, we have employed a structured approach to evaluate and rank them based on specific criteria.

The primary concept driving the selection process is to identify and analyze those militaries that demonstrated exceptional capabilities in war or conflict, had significant impact on their respective societies, and left lasting legacies for future generations. This concept emerged out of the understanding that military forces have played vital roles across different civilizations, not only in defense but also as catalysts for socio-political development and transformation.

The criteria for judging what constitutes a great military force has been refined over time in response to historical accounts, expert opinions, and comparative analyses. By considering multiple dimensions of military prowess, we aim to create an unbiased evaluation encompassing various aspects ranging from operational readiness and combat efficiency to technological innovations and leadership.

The following criteria have been developed to determine the significance and greatness of various military forces throughout history:

1. **Organizational Capability:** This criterion assesses how well a military force was organized and structured. The degree of organization often indicates how efficiently resources were managed and deployed in times of war or peace, which is crucial for maintaining its operational effectiveness.
2. **Leadership and Command Structure:** The quality of leadership can sometimes make or break an army's success on

the battlefield. Thus, we considered factors such as strategic vision, tactical acumen, adaptability in varying situations, as well as leadership hierarchy that facilitated effective decision-making.

3. **Force Size and Effectiveness:** The size alone does not define a military's prowess, but there is no denying that substantial forces have shaped history. Therefore, we must examine not only the sheer size but also the effectiveness of personnel – a force's ability to train, equip, and maintain its troops and support system.

4. **Technological Advancements:** The use of technology has always played a crucial role in determining military superiority. An effective force would be able to acquire, incorporate, and utilize cutting-edge technology for improving its capabilities.

5. **Geographical Influence and Expansion:** It is important to consider how much territory a military managed to conquer or control throughout its existence, including the defensive fortifications it maintained. This serves as an indicator of its strategic reach and operational considerations.

6. **Legacy and Cultural Impact:** Finally, military forces that left everlasting imprints on the societies they served or conquered must be assessed based on their contributions to shaping cultural identity, national narratives, and historical legacies.

These six criteria were employed in tandem when deciding upon our selection of the 100 greatest militaries throughout history. Moreover, they offer a comprehensive framework that accounts for various aspects that have contributed to the formation of what is considered "great" in terms of historical military might.

As we journey through these pages and explore the exceptional military forces featured in this book, readers are encouraged to examine each case study through these lenses. By gaining deeper insights into what made these armies exceptional in such diverse contexts, we can reflect upon how they continue to influence modern warfare and contemporary societies long after their historical timeframes have passed.

The Significance of Military History

Military history is the study of armies, navies, and other armed forces in relation to the historical backdrop of societies and civilizations. It attempts to analyze warfare's impact on cultural, social, and political developments. One of the primary reasons for studying military history is that it provides a context for understanding the emergence of nations and empires. The rise and fall of these entities are often closely tied to their military prowess and conquests. By examining past military events, one can better comprehend how nations are shaped and transformed by warfare. Notable examples include the rise of Rome, which was built upon centuries of military success against various adversaries such as Carthage in the Punic Wars or barbarian tribes during its expansionist era.

Another crucial aspect that highlights the significance of military history is its influence on technological advancements. Warfare has consistently driven invention throughout human history as competing powers sought an edge over their rivals. Developments in engineering, metallurgy, medicine, communications, transportation, and even agriculture have shaped domestic life as well as the battlefield. For example, World War II saw trailblazing innovations in jet engines and computing technology that would eventually propel mankind into space and revolutionize modern society.

Moreover, military history allows us to appreciate the origins of strategic thinking which is vital to modern diplomacy and international relations. Many principles underlying contemporary political strategies have evolved from historical wartime situations. Great tacticians such as Sun Tzu in ancient China or Carl von Clausewitz in 18th century Europe continue to influence modern philosophies on war strategy and politics. Studying their writings can offer valuable insights into decision-making processes involved in conflict resolution and managing international tensions.

Lessons from military history also serve as a foundation for ethical and humanitarian discussions. The study of past conflicts provides a range of perspectives on morality and the just conduct in times of war. As human civilizations have matured, so has our understanding of what is considered right or wrong when faced with the inherent violence of warfare. By examining historical events, we become more aware of the complexities involved with issues such as war crimes, human rights violations, and responsibilities towards civilians in conflict zones.

Furthermore, understanding military history supports cultural literacy as it frequently intersects with other scholarly disciplines. The armed forces often played a significant role in shaping the arts, religion, and architecture throughout history. Examining the military's impact on these aspects can significantly broaden one's perspective on historic events.

Finally, the significance of military history is also evident in collective memory and national identity formation. Societies often construct narratives around pivotal battles or prominent military figures to represent their values and aspirations. Celebrations such as Independence Day or armistice commemorations serve as an opportunity for nations to reflect on their past achievements and look towards future developments.

Ancient Era

Overview of Influential Ancient Military Forces

The development and organization of military forces have been crucial in shaping cultures, power dynamics, and the world as we know it today. Among the countless armies that have existed, three ancient military forces stand out as particularly influential examples: the Roman Empire, the Persian Empire, and Ancient Chinese Armies.

Roman Empire (c. 27 BC-476 AD)

The Roman Empire is often considered one of history's greatest military powers. From its inception during the reign of Augustus to its fall in 476 AD, the Romans demonstrated exceptional skill and ingenuity on and off the battlefield.

1. **Legions:** The backbone of Rome's military might was its legions - disciplined and highly skilled soldiers that were versatile and capable of enduring harsh conditions. A typical legion consisted of around 5,000 heavy infantrymen (legionaries), which were divided into smaller units called centuries (80-100 men) led by a centurion.
2. **Siege Warfare:** The Romans excelled at siege warfare, utilizing elaborate constructions such as battering rams, catapults, and siege towers to break into enemy fortifications effectively.
3. **Military Architecture**: Formidable military infrastructure played a vital role in securing Rome's expansive territories. Impressive forts dotted strategically across the empire acted as fortified centers for garrisons while an extensive network of roads facilitated lightning-fast troop movement.

4. **Pax Romana:** Roman military success resulted in imperial stability, leading to an unprecedented 200-year-long period referred to as "Pax Romana" or Roman Peace.

Persian Empire (550 BC-330 BC)

Founded by Cyrus the Great after conquering Medes in 550 BC, the Persian Empire developed into an astounding superpower with well-organized and formidable armies that enabled ambitious expansionist aims.

1. **Immortals:** Among the Empire's famed soldiers were the Immortals - an elite force of 10,000 heavily armed infantrymen named due to their constant replenishment to maintain their numbers.
2. **Cavalry:** The Persian Empire was one of the first ancient powers to emphasize the importance of horse-bound warfare. This impressive cavalry allowed them to conduct lightning-fast, shock-and-awe tactics that left enemies unable to respond.
3. **Logistics and Communication:** The efficient administration of the empire was maintained by a highly effective logistics and communication system that allowed for rapid movement of troops and messages. Notably, the Persian messenger system was known for its reliability and speed that even surpassed that of the later Roman Empire.
4. **Persian Tolerance:** By adopting tolerant policies towards conquered people, including recognizing local customs and systems, Persia mitigated resentment from subjects which reduced internal strife and potential rebellion.

Ancient Chinese Armies (c.1122 BC-221 BC)

Ancient China saw the rise of sophisticated military forces as various states vied for dominance during the tumultuous period known as Warring States.

1. **The Art of War:** Sun Tzu's renowned treatise on military strategy, "The Art of War," is thought to have greatly shaped ancient Chinese warfare with insights on conflict resolution, deception tactics, flexibility in exercises, and adapting opponent weaknesses.
2. **Crossbow Prowess:** Chinese armies made extensive use of state-of-the-art crossbows with startling accuracy, range, and power rivaling any modern-day firearm.
3. **Terracotta Army:** Qin Shi Huang's famous Terracotta Army demonstrates the scale and sophistication of ancient Chinese military organization with an estimated 8,000 soldiers and even more horses and chariots found in Emperor Qin's mausoleum.

The influence exerted by these ancient military forces is still apparent in our modern world: Roman legions remain an archetype for professional and disciplined armies; Persian tolerance and communication strategies offer lessons on intercultural cohesion; and Chinese strategic insights from The Art of War have become universal and time-tested wisdom for military enthusiasts and scholars. These iconic military forces continue to inspire us to look back in history to understand the human story, technology, warfare, and the challenges of organizing vast empires.

Key Strategies, Technologies, And Battles

One of the most significant military strategies of antiquity was the use of the phalanx formation. This highly organized and disciplined arrangement involved soldiers, or hoplites, standing shoulder to shoulder in tight rows with their shields interlocked to form a sturdy shield wall. They would also wield long spears or pikes to fend off enemy infantry and cavalry. This approach was employed primarily by Ancient Greek city-states such as Sparta and Athens and contributed greatly to their military success on the battlefield.

The use of archers in ancient warfare was another crucial strategy. Civilizations such as the Persians and Egyptians used archers as potent long-range weapons able to harass and weaken enemy forces before engaging in direct combat. Archers required considerable skill to use effectively, but they could provide decisive advantages when utilized correctly.

Technology also played a fundamental role in the development of ancient militaries. For example, during this era, the Romans engineered some impressive advancements such as their formidable siege engines like battering rams, catapults, and ballistae. These tools allowed them to overcome formidable defenses of fortified cities which would have been nearly impossible solely with infantry.

One notable battle illustrating this point is the Siege of Alesia in 52 BC, where Julius Caesar's Roman legions surrounded a Gallic stronghold led by Vercingetorix. The Romans built an extensive network of fortifications around Alesia which included ditches, walls, watchtowers, traps and utilized state-of-the-art weapons designed to assemble rapidly. After months of fighting heavily against both internal defenders and external relief forces seeking to break the siege, Caesar emerged victorious, effectively marking the end of unified Gallic resistance against Rome.

In ancient warfare, the invention of the chariot was another groundbreaking technological advancement. Chariots allowed for greater speed and mobility in battle, which could be decisive when used tactically to exploit flanks and weaknesses in the enemy line. The Egyptians, Hittites, and Assyrians were among the most adept at utilizing chariots in battle.

This advantage can be seen during the Battle of Kadesh in 1274 BC between the Egyptians led by Pharaoh Ramesses II and the Hittites under King Muwatalli II. This conflict is regarded as one of the largest chariot battles ever fought, with both sides deploying thousands of sophisticated chariots to seize tactical control over a region on the banks of River Orontes. Although the outcome of this battle remains disputed, it showcased the power and influence of chariot warfare.

The ancient naval warfare sphere also experienced notable developments during this time. The Greeks, Persians, and Carthaginians each utilized their navies to project and protect their territorial interests on water. One standout battle is the Battle of Salamis that took place in 480 BC between a massive Persian fleet led by King Xerxes I against an allied Greek fleet under Themistocles.

With deep understanding of geography and superior tactical sense, Themistocles engaged Persian ships within a tight strait off Greece's coast where their vast numbers couldn't be fully exploited. Using smaller, more maneuverable vessels called triremes, equipped with rams for striking enemy ships, Greek forces managed to achieve a pivotal victory despite being vastly outnumbered - all thanks to naval strategy development.

Relationship Between Political Powers and Military Might

As empires expanded and kingdoms rose from obscurity, the wielders of these twin forces would most often determine the destiny of their subjects. At the heart of ancient civilizations lay their rulers' unyielding pursuit for consolidation of power. Political figures often relied on military prowess to expand their territories, maintain internal stability, and ward off adversaries seeking to usurp their positions. It was not uncommon for an ambitious general to become a benevolent monarch by virtue of his military achievements, illustrating how inextricably linked political ascendancy was with martial prowess.

The rise and fall of the world-renowned Achaemenid Persian Empire under Cyrus the Great best illustrates this dynamic. Entering into an alliance with Babylon, Cyrus focused his early campaigns on conquering surrounding territories such as Lydia and Babylon itself. Thanks to his adept militaristic strategies and sheer willpower, he effectively expanded Persian territory across three continents – a feat never seen before. The hierarchical satrapy system that propelled Persia to greatness further underscored how intrinsically politics and military power were interwoven; each satrap governed a province while providing troops for imperial expansion or defense.

Another shining example from antiquity is Rome's ascent from a city-state to one of history's most iconic empires spanning Europe, Africa, and Asia. While Rome's republican government structure initially provided checks and balances against military abuses of power, it ultimately succumbed when generals like Gaius Marius and Lucius Cornelius Sulla pushed boundaries with their legions at their backs. Arguably, it was Julius Caesar's military conquests in Gaul that propelled his political career to prominence, culminating in his eventual seizure of power. This move darkened Rome's skyline, steadily transforming the republic into an empire dominated by an emperor vested with unparalleled military and political power.

As politicians and generals amassed both military and political clout, they directed their increased authority towards infrastructure projects, propelling societies to reach new developmental heights. The Great Wall of China, one of the world's most monumental architectural achievements, emerged from this fusion. Under Emperor Qin Shi Huang's unified rule, the enormous project unified and protected China from incursions by northern invaders, reflecting the delicate balance between strategy, engineering, and political ambitions.

However, the merging of politics with military might was not solely concentrated on grandiose missions. Through conquests and expansion, emerging empires assimilated different cultures into their fold and promulgated diverse practices across their territories. This phenomenon fostered a melting pot of cultures that encouraged cross-pollination of ideas in various spheres – philosophy, science, art, and literature. The Hellenistic era following Alexander the Great's conquests is a testimony to this cultural diffusion with mathematician Euclid in Alexandria and polymath Archimedes in Syracuse standing as shining examples.

Inevitably, this marriage between military capacity and political authority would lead to conflicts when another civilization coveted what their neighbors had achieved. Ancient history brims with tales of brutal wars fought on this pretext – the Greco-Persian Wars bear witness to the enduring tenacity borne by opposing civilizations protecting their sovereignty while vying for dominance.

Despite its grounding in antiquity, the fusion between martial and political power continues to fascinate us today as we scour through history books documenting remarkable feats accomplished by statesmen wielding swords alongside quills. This study should serve as an enlightening reminder that the same forces that shaped ancient human history continue to reverberate with indelible consequences for our world today.

Ancient Near East and Far East Militaries

Exploration Of Military Powers

Within the vast expanse of military history, several ancient civilizations stand out as remarkable examples of unparalleled military prowess. Among these, the Babylonians, Assyrians, and Hittites have each demonstrated incredible skill and ingenuity in the strategies deployed during conquests.

Babylonians: The Rulers of Mesopotamia

The Babylonian Empire was situated in Mesopotamia, a land known as the cradle of civilization. From its founding in the early 19th century BCE, various ruling dynasties emerged before Hammurabi united the area in 1759 BCE. The Babylonians were skilled diplomats who employed alliances to fortify their defense. However, their greatest asset was their robust army.

Babylonian warriors were well-versed in infantry tactics utilizing bronze weapons like spears, swords, and daggers. The introduction of chariots enhanced their fighting capabilities, allowing them to strike with swift precision. Archers used composite bows made from layers of wood and sinew; these formidable weapons offered an incredible range and devastating impact on enemy forces. Siege warfare was also a vital part of their military approach; battering rams and siege towers allowed them to overcome enemy fortifications.

Assyrians: Masters of War

The fertile lands along the Tigris River set the stage for another resilient group – the Assyrians. They stood out among ancient military forces due to their innovative tactics and technology. The Assyrian Empire reached its zenith during the reigns of Tiglath-Pileser III (reigned 745-727 BCE), Sargon II (reigned 722-705 BCE), Sennacherib (reigned 705-681 BCE), Esarhaddon (reigned 681-669 BCE), and Ashurbanipal (reigned 669-631 BCE).

Assyrian soldiers were disciplined, courageous, and cruel. They used iron weapons, unlike their contemporaries who relied on bronze. This strategic advantage allowed the Assyrians to inflict greater damage on enemy troops and fortifications. Like the Babylonians, the Assyrians employed infantry, chariots, and archers in their battles, but they expanded on these tactics.

Horse-mounted warriors provided speed and flexibility to Assyrian forces that enabled them to outmaneuver opponents. Their advanced arsenal included slingers whose projectiles could fell a soldier from afar or reduce a city wall to rubble in days. Assyrians also specialized in psychological warfare, deliberately instilling fear in their enemies by spreading tales of their mercilessness. This reputation often led adversaries to surrender without battle.

Hittites: The Iron Warriors

In Anatolia (modern-day Turkey), the Hittite Empire thrived from around 1600 BCE to 1200 BCE. It is believed that they were among the first civilizations to utilize iron for weaponry and tools, giving them a vital advantage over other regional powers.

The Hittite military was meticulously organized into various units such as infantrymen, charioteers, archers, and support staff like blacksmiths and armorers. Their infantry was heavily armed with large shields, spears for close combat, and curved swords or sickle-shaped blades for slicing through opponents' defenses.

The Hittites' deadliest weapon was their mastery of chariot warfare. They constructed lighter chariots steered by a single warrior; atypically accommodating three soldiers – a driver, an archer, and a protective shield-bearer who repelled enemy attacks in the heat of battle.

For defense strategies, Hittite fortresses featured thick walls with sturdy watchtowers. Their unique architectural design incorporated gates placed between staggering walls; this layout stalled enemy advancements allowing defenders to counteract besieging forces.

Though the Babylonians, Assyrians, and Hittites may have thrived in different periods and locations, their military achievements remain remarkable today. These civilizations revolutionized warfare through technological advancements, tactical innovations, and relentless discipline. Their strategic prowess not only facilitated the expansion of vast territories but also contributed significantly to how militaries continued to develop long after their decline.

Early Chinese Dynastic Armies and Their Warfare Tactics

Ancient China's military history traces back to the early dynastic period, where innovation in military tactics and strategies decided the fate of kings and emperors. The Shang Dynasty (1600-1046 BC) boasts one of the oldest examples of an organized military force in ancient China. The Shang army was predominantly composed of infantry, utilizing bronze weapons for combat such as the Ge (dagger-ax), spears, and bows. The Shang commanders deployed their forces with great precision and coordination, achieving impressive victories over their enemies.

One crucial factor in Shang Dynasty warfare was their ability to create a vast network of noble-led chariot units. The nobles and their elite troops would charge into battle with groups of three chariots that formed a fast-moving strike force. These units were highly effective against enemy infantry formations, breaking through lines and causing chaos on the battlefield.

The Zhou Dynasty (1046–256 BC) came next, inheriting many of the Shang Dynasty's tactics while also introducing new strategies to improve its fighting capabilities. Most notably, they developed extensive cavalry units that augmented their chariot forces further. These mounted troops could respond rapidly to threats with speed and maneuverability while wielding long-range weapons such as halberds or composite bows. Additionally, they reinforced their defenses with formidable armies making use of crossbowmen, pikemen, and heavily armored infantry.

A significant tactical evolution in Zhou Dynasty warfare was the establishment of the 'Mandate of Heaven,' which linked war with divine approval. The rulers believed that a just emperor had divine favor on his side, leading to victory in battle. This concept also engendered staunch loyalty among soldiers, further buoying their morale and discipline on the battlefield.

The Spring and Autumn Period (770–476 BC) saw numerous conflicts as states vied for supremacy. Arguably, the most significant advancement during this time was the phalanx formation consisting of shielded infantry wielding long spears in tight linear unit formations. This tactic offered greater protection against enemy attacks, primarily when soldiers worked in unison to maintain their line integrity.

Enter Sun Tzu, a renowned military strategist and philosopher who lived during this period. Author of 'The Art of War,' Sun Tzu emphasized the importance of deception, flexibility, and adaptability on the battlefield. By following his principles, such as using terrain advantageously and selecting when to engage judiciously, commanders could outthink their opponents and secure victory with minimal losses.

Towards the end of the Spring and Autumn Period came the Warring States Period (475–221 BC) – an era defined by extended warfare among various competing states. Qin Shi Huang's unification of China happened through a combination of military might and diplomatic alliances. The Qin Dynasty's success relied on its adoption of Legalism, a philosophy focused on strict adherence to laws, discipline, and order. Drawing upon previous dynastic wisdoms, Qin armies extensively utilized sophisticated tactics such as encirclement maneuvers, logistical supply lines, and scorched-earth strategies.

The Qin Dynasty's success was short-lived; however, it paved the way for the Han Dynasty (202 BC–220 AD) – a golden era for Chinese military development. The Han army prioritized technology as a cornerstone for its success in warfare; most notably witnessed through their usage of advanced crossbows that could penetrate armor at impressive distances. Nation-spanning projects like the Great Wall highlighted Han leadership's strategic foresight in utilizing structures that would protect against invasions from Xiongnu nomads for centuries.

The Rise of The Ancient Japanese Samurai Class

The ancient Japanese samurai class emerged as one of the most formidable and respected groups in the history of warfare. The establishment of the samurai class traces back to the late Heian Period (794-1185), a time of political turmoil in Japan. With a weakened central government, regional lords or daimyos sought to consolidate power by relying on their own private armies for security and territorial expansion. This, in turn, led to the formation of various warrior families who provided their military services in exchange for land and resources.

The term "samurai" itself derives from the word "saburau," which means "to serve," highlighting their role as loyal servants to their respective lords. Initially, they were highly skilled mounted archers and horsemen who specialized in guerrilla tactics and hit-and-run warfare. Over time, however, they evolved into an elite class of warriors whose prowess extended beyond their martial abilities.

Throughout the Kamakura Period (1185-1333), the samurai class gained further distinction due to major shifts in Japan's political landscape. The victorious samurai leader Minamoto no Yoritomo established the Kamakura shogunate – a military government that would rule Japan for nearly 150 years. This signified a monumental change in power dynamics, transitioning from a civilian-led aristocracy to a government dominated by the warrior class.

Under Shogun Yoritomo's rule, the samurai's value system evolved to adopt strict codes of conduct called bushido – a set of virtues emphasizing loyalty, honor, self-discipline, and devotion to duty. The fusion of martial prowess and moral principles made the samurai both a feared and revered figure in Japanese society.

The rise of the samurai class is also closely tied to their iconic weaponry and armor. Most notably, the katana – a curved, single-edged sword – became synonymous with the samurai identity. Combining artistry, craftsmanship, and cutting-edge technology, this weapon was developed in response to the need for a versatile yet lethal battlefield instrument. The distinctive curvature of the sword allowed for quick, powerful strikes capable of penetrating enemy armor.

The samurai's armor was likewise designed for both functionality and aesthetics. Known as 'yoroi,' it was composed of lacquered iron plates laced together with silk or leather cords. The helmet, or 'kabuto,' often featured a distinctive crest called a 'mon.' The elaborate designs of the samurai's armor not only protected its wearer but also served as an expression of individuality and status.

Over time, the samurai class began to garner influence in Japan's cultural sphere. They were patrons of arts such as calligraphy, poetry, tea ceremony, and Noh theater – interests that extended beyond their martial role. However, the waning power of the shogunate system in favor of the imperial court led to a gradual decline in the samurai's status during Japan's peaceful Edo Period (1603-1868). Their role as warriors diminished with the absence of major conflicts and by the end of this period, they often served as bureaucrats or advisors instead.

The ultimate downfall of the samurai class culminated during Japan's Meiji Restoration (1868-1912). With rapid modernization and westernization taking precedence over traditional values, Emperor Meiji abolished the samurai's rights to bear arms and wear swords in public. Consequently, this transition relegated them to historical symbols rather than active players in Japan's military sphere.

Medieval and Renaissance Militaries

Military Powers of the Middle Ages and Renaissance Period

The annals of military history are filled with remarkable tales, from the remarkably advanced tactics employed by ancient empires to the modern developments in warfare. One cannot truly understand these historic milestones without exploring the military achievements and innovations during the Middle Ages and Renaissance period. The Mongol Empire, Ottoman Empire, and European powers each left an indelible mark in this fascinating era.

In the 12th century, the Mongol Empire, under the leadership of Genghis Khan, began a series of conquests that would continue for centuries, eventually forming one of history's largest empires. At its peak, it spanned from Eastern Europe to East Asia, bridging various cultures and peoples. Perhaps the most notable thing about the Mongol military was their unparalleled proficiency in cavalry warfare. Combining horsemanship and archery skills with lightning-fast mobility, they created a formidable force that could swiftly overwhelm their enemies.

The Mongols' technology included the composite bow—a highly efficient long-range weapon capable of penetrating armor from considerable distances. Their battle tactics relied on speed, flexibility, and efficiency: They employed feints and misdirection to outmaneuver less agile opponents, carefully studied enemy strategies to exploit any weaknesses, and used psychological warfare rumormongering to sow discord among enemy ranks.

As they expanded their empire through conquests, the Mongols adopted new techniques from conquered cultures and incorporated them into their own military strategies. This adaptability allowed them to assimilate rapidly within foreign territories—an important factor that contributed greatly to their empire's growth.

Meanwhile, in Europe during the Middle Ages, feudalism laid the foundation for military organization. As fiefdoms expanded and coalesced into nations, local lords raised private armies to protect their lands from both internal rivals and external threats. European knights became symbols of medieval warfare—equipped with plate armor that provided great protection in close combat, these elite warriors would go on to form the backbone of many European armies.

As Europe began to recover from the Mongol invasions, military innovations such as infantry-based pike formations and gunpowder weaponry helped level the playing field against the once-dominant Mongol cavalry. The major players in Europe—including England, France, and Spain—each developed their own distinct military tactics, but cooperation among nations through alliances and trade played a crucial role in shaping the continent's balance of power.

In the mid-15th century, the Ottoman Empire emerged as one of the most powerful military forces of its time. Expanding into Europe and across much of western Asia, it ultimately managed to overthrow Constantinople, the mighty capital of Byzantium. Among its most celebrated achievements was the development of unique Janissary infantry units—a highly trained force comprised of abducted Christian children taken from their families during periodic "blood tax" levies.

Janissaries were rigorously trained from a young age in harsh conditions that honed their skills in discipline, obedience, and weaponry. At their height, these elite units established a fearsome reputation that resonated throughout the region. Building on early gunpowder weapons introduced by Europe during this period, the Ottomans refined and mastered cannons—transforming them into a mainstay of their military.

A significant factor in Ottoman Empire military successes was its ability to marshal resources. Utilizing centralized bureaucratic administration systems borrowed from Persian traditions, they efficiently organized numerous campaigns across vast distances while maintaining supply lines for their troops—an impressive achievement for any empire.

Highlighting Advancements in Weaponry, Tactics, and Conquests

Weaponry evolved considerably, which led to new tactics and ultimately reshaped the way wars were fought and won. Weaponry advancements during the Medieval and Renaissance periods included crossbows, longbows, firearms, artillery cannons, and improved armor. The crossbow was a remarkable innovation that originated in China around the 4th century BC but gained widespread popularity in medieval Europe. With its potential to penetrate chainmail armor and release bolts at extraordinary speed from a relatively far distance, it became an excellent weapon for both foot soldiers and mounted knights.

Another powerful weapon of this era was the longbow. It had a longer range than the crossbow and could be shot more rapidly but required greater strength and skill to use effectively. Longbows played a crucial role in many decisive battles such as the Battle of Agincourt in 1415.

Gunpowder weaponry brought about radical changes in warfare during these times as well. Firearms like arquebuses became common infantry weapons toward the end of the medieval period. This marks a significant shift away from traditional archery, giving infantry flexibility and lethal capability on the battlefield.

Cannons evolved during this period as well; they went from being small stone or iron balls used primarily for siege purposes to large bronze or cast-iron projectiles capable of leveling city walls or even smashing enemy ships at sea with astonishing power.

Advancements in armor also transformed warfare during these periods. Plate armor crafted from steel plates provided knights with superior protection against various forms of combat weapons. This enhancement significantly shaped warfare by placing heavier emphasis on shock tactics used by cavalry and allied infantry to break through enemy lines.

New tactics emerged in response to these weapon and armor innovations. Previously, many battles were won by heavily armored knights charging headlong into the opposing infantry. However, as crossbows and longbows became more powerful and prevalent, their effectiveness waned. Tactics adapted by incorporating infantry and archers in combined arms units that were more versatile on the battlefield. Shield barriers/walls were employed to protect infantry, while longbows and crossbows targeted the opposition from a safe distance.

As firearms became more common, battle strategies began prioritizing controlled infantry formations to obliterate the enemy's forces with volleys of fire. Gunpowder artillery also caused shifts in siege warfare tactics; stone walls could no longer withstand prolonged bombardments from powerful cannons.

Military conquests during this era evoke images of valor, chivalry, and ruthless ambition. In the medieval period, William the Conqueror successfully invaded England in 1066, leading to centuries of Norman influence on English culture and politics. Genghis Khan established the Mongol Empire by conquering vast territories across Asia throughout the 13th century.

The Renaissance saw the unification of Spain under Ferdinand II and Isabella I following their successful conquest of Granada in 1492. This marked not only a momentous victory for Spanish Catholicism but also set the stage for Spain's domination over much of the Americas later.

Other significant conquests during this period include the rise of the Ottoman Empire, particularly during Suleiman the Magnificent's reign in the 16th century. Under his rule, Ottomans expanded deep into Europe, further solidifying their position as a dominant global power.

Importance Of Religion and Chivalry in Shaping Medieval Warfare

Religion played a prominent role in medieval warfare by providing moral justifications for armed conflict and rallying support from various social strata. The Christian church wielded immense authority in medieval Europe, making its endorsement or condemnation of military actions crucial. One of the most famous instances where religion served as a decisive impetus for war was the Crusades. Between 1096 and 1291, a series of holy wars sanctioned by the church sought to retake Jerusalem from Muslim control.

The Crusades profoundly impacted the outlook on warfare among European nobility and commoners alike. Religious motivations justified war both internationally (as a religious duty) and domestically (to settle disputes without church condemnation). Crusaders who demonstrated unwavering faith were promised spiritual rewards and forgiveness from sins, an enticing prospect in an era of fervent piety.

Simultaneously, religious institutions such as monastic orders maintained a strong military presence throughout medieval Europe. The Knights Templar, Hospitallers, and Teutonic Knights were not only religious communities but also professional fighting forces that were called upon to defend Christian territories against heathen armies. As a result, they became embodiments of martial valor steeped in religion.

Chivalry was another influential factor in shaping medieval warfare; it represented an unwritten code of conduct that bound knights to virtues such as bravery, loyalty, honor, and respect. Originating in the 11th century, chivalry reached its apex during the 12th and 13th centuries, reflecting a changing social landscape that saw the rise of a noble warrior class. Chivalry's core principles necessitated that knights protect the weak, serve their lords faithfully, and maintain an unblemished sense of honor.

This emphasis on chivalric honor played out on the battlefield, where knights sought glory and distinction in ways that influenced warfare tactics. The spectacle of single combat between knights before a battle became an iconic practice and reflected the importance of individual prowess. Furthermore, ransom for captured noblemen allowed for stories of knightly generosity even among enemies - a peculiar but common dynamic in medieval warfare.

Chivalry also shaped the ethos of military orders such as the previously mentioned Knights Templar and Hospitallers. Their founders aspired to blend religious fervor with martial prowess and heroic dedication to a sacred cause. This fusion resulted in uniquely chivalrous organizations ready to defend Christianity with sword and shield.

While religion and chivalry proved significant in shaping medieval warfare's character, both concepts had limitations that treatment of non-combatants exposed. Crusading campaigns often brought about brutal treatment of civilian populations considered enemies of Christendom. Chivalric honor held little meaning for common soldiers who bore the brunt of combat and had no chance for personal glory or ransom.

Early Modern Period Militaries in Europe

Examination Of Military Developments During The 18th Century

The 18th century was marked by profound transformations in the landscape of warfare and military developments. As armies expanded, tactics evolved, and technology advanced, conflicts such as the Napoleonic Wars, the rise of the British Empire, and the formidable Prussian Army revolutionized modern warfare.

The stage for these military developments was set in Europe where alliances shifted, and cities became battlegrounds. The increasing professionalism of soldiers signaled a departure from earlier centuries which were dominated by militias or mercenaries. This period saw the emergence of standing armies with highly trained and well-equipped personnel.

One key development in this era was the use of line infantry tactics. Armies formed lines three deep, with successive ranks firing volleys and then being replaced by new rows ready to fire. This method allowed large numbers of soldiers to engage in battle simultaneously, maximizing fighting power. The improved accuracy of firearms, especially rifling in barrels, facilitated this tactic.

The Napoleonic Wars were emblematic of this transformation. These conflicts erupted between 1803 and 1815 and involved cordial European powers striving to contain Napoleon Bonaparte's expansionist ambitions. Napoleon was able to mobilize resources across his empire, assembling one of the most potent fighting forces in history. His Grande Armée incorporated conscription on a vast scale to sustain a relentless series of campaigns across Europe.

As a tactical innovator, Napoleon made expert use of cavalry and artillery to achieve rapid victories against his enemies. His strategy of concentrating forces at decisive points on the battlefield involved moving them quickly using extensive road networks established during his reign. On top of massing forces for overwhelming strikes, he combined political propaganda with military action to erode enemy morale.

During this period, the British Empire also emerged as a global superpower with an extensive colonial empire spanning every continent. Key factors in its military success included improvements in logistics, doctrine, and organization. The Royal Navy became the preeminent seafaring force of the era, dominating maritime trade and securing colonial territories.

The British East India Company played a pivotal role in securing these territories under the British crown. By raising native Indian troops under British leadership, this force successfully subjugated large swathes of South Asia and laid the foundations for direct colonial rule.

At the same time, Britain's strategic focus was upon maintaining its position on the balance of power in Europe. To this end, it pursued policies such as subsidizing other European nations in their struggles against France. British forces were relied upon to provide vital naval support during campaigns against Napoleon, culminating in the decisive victory at the Battle of Waterloo in 1815.

In parallel to these conflicts, another European power was also making crucial strides on the battleground: Prussia. The Prussian Army pioneered significant advancements in organization, leadership, and recruitment. Under King Frederick William I, Prussia adopted a highly efficient administrative system that emphasized discipline and order throughout its ranks.

Frederick William's son, Frederick II (Frederick the Great), built on his father's groundwork to forge one of history's most formidable fighting forces. Known for his tactical nous and relentless pursuit of victory regardless of odds, Frederick led Prussia through numerous victories against Austria and other opponents during the Seven Years' War.

The Prussian military model was influential across Europe. Its strengths lay in its ability to rapidly mobilize forces so that its adversaries struggled with demanding expeditionary warfare. This model focused on flexibility over rigid hierarchy and featured excellent coordination among different branches of its armed forces.

Industrial Revolution and its Impact

As European militaries evolved during the early modern period, the impacts of these changes on armed conflict became increasingly apparent. One of the most critical factors influencing warfare during this period was the consolidation and centralization of state power. The increased revenue generated by wealthier, more extensive, and more complex economies allowed European governments to finance substantial standing armies with much greater ease. These professional military forces were equipped with increasingly sophisticated weapons and technology, laying the groundwork for a new era of military strategy and tactics.

The industrial revolution impacted European militaries through both direct and indirect means. At its core, the revolution focused on manufacturing technologies that spurred advancements in weaponry. Early European militaries took advantage of these innovations; firearms began to replace traditional weapons like pikes and muskets.

One of the most recognizable developments in this field was the introduction of rifles with grooved barrels, known as rifling. These new firearms provided soldiers with enhanced accuracy over their predecessors, allowing them to engage enemies at longer distances. Moreover, improvements in gunpowder resulted in more reliable firepower from artillery pieces such as cannonadesm which could now shoot heavy shells filled with explosive materials effectively.

Naval warfare underwent similarly transformative changes. The rise of coal power led to iron-hulled steamships replacing contemporaneous sailing vessels made from wood and canvas. The increased speed capabilities made these vessels superior to their predecessors as they did not rely on wind; this dramatically altered naval combat strategies, leading to a geopolitical shift in which maritime powers fought for control over strategic resources like coal ports.

Transporting troops had become much more efficient thanks to innovations in infrastructure and transit. The development of railroad systems enabled armies to move vast distances in significantly less time, ensuring rapid mobilization and deployment of personnel, equipment, and supplies. Nations that were early adopters of this technology were granted significant advantages over their rivals, as demonstrated by the Prussian military victories during the Franco-Prussian War in 1870-1871.

The industrial revolution also prompted major developments in communication technology, which proved to be instrumental for military planning and decision-making. Telegraph systems allowed for nearly instant long-distance communication, drastically reducing information lag between headquarters and troops on the front lines. This newfound ability to adapt to changing combat situations made communication an essential component of military operations.

Beyond innovations directly related to warfare, the industrial revolution had profound implications for the broader European social landscape. Populations grew rapidly in response to increased agricultural efficiency and urban living conditions. Large urban centers provided fertile grounds for the militarization of their populations, as the vast pool of citizens offered ample manpower for military recruitment.

Industrialization also stimulated the spread of ideologies such as nationalism and imperialism. The rise of fervent national pride contributed significantly to European nations' appetites for expansion and conquest, forging new alliances and rivalries in an increasingly interconnected world. This competition led to both arms races and colonialism, with empires seeking out new territories in pursuit of resources that could fuel their burgeoning industrial economies.

Despite its numerous innovations and advancements, the industrial revolution's influence over the militaries of Early Modern Europe was not without cost. Technological advancements often came with social struggles and upheavals as individuals struggled to adapt; armies faced a myriad of challenges related to training soldiers for modern combat techniques and strategies. New forms of weaponry made conflict increasingly devastating, demonstrated most horrifically during World War I's brutal trench warfare.

As new innovations in technology and industry changed the way Europeans viewed themselves and the world, their militaries adapted accordingly, transforming the very nature of armed conflict. This ever-evolving landscape paved the way for some of history's most significant military campaigns, proving that innovation and power could be as bloody and tragic as it was transformative and triumphant. The echoes of these changes still reverberate in modern warfare, reminding us of a time when Europe was grappling with an entirely new world order.

The Infamous Pirate Age and Privateering

Spanning from the late 17th century to the early 18th century, this extraordinary period saw daring and cunning seafarers challenging the established political and economic order on both land and sea. In the waters of the Caribbean Sea, Atlantic Ocean, Gulf of Mexico, Indian Ocean, and even as far as Southeast Asia, pirates spread fear and terror across vast maritime territories. These skilled navigators were not bound to any nation or king but pursued their ambitions through ruthlessness and brutal efficiency. Pirate ships sailed under the Jolly Roger – a flag emblazoned with skull and crossbones designed to conjure dread in any who beheld it. Pirates targeted merchant vessels laden with valuable cargo such as gold, silver, spices, textiles, tobacco – anything they could convert into immense wealth.

The Golden Age of Piracy is often associated with notorious figures such as Blackbeard (Edward Teach), Captain Kidd (William Kidd), and Calico Jack (John Rackham). These individuals became infamous not only for their thieving exploits but also for their flamboyant personalities that seemed to be drawn from epic tales of heroism and villainy rather than historical facts. Blackbeard in particular would become one of history's most fearsome pirates, known for his wiry mass of facial hair which he weaved slow-burning fuses into. Smoking like some firebrand demon as he boarded enemy ships filled those facing him with abject terror.

However, while piracy was deemed unlawful by most societies during this age, it is essential to distinguish these outlaws from privateers. Privateers were armed vessels operating under the commission of a host nation, attacking and seizing enemy ships during times of war. Essentially, they were sanctioned pirates, investing their skills in the service of empires such as Britain, Spain, France, and the Dutch Republic. Because of their effectiveness against enemy shipping, they became an important aspect of naval warfare and economic competition between these colonial powers.

Governments issued letters of marque – legal documents authorizing privateers to target enemy commerce and rewarded them with a share of the captured spoils. In fact, some historical figures such as Sir Francis Drake and Sir Walter Raleigh began their seafaring careers as privateers. With their state-sanctioned exploits against the Spanish Empire, they became heroes in Elizabethan England – both earning knighthoods while simultaneously infuriating their enemies.

Despite the romantic depictions of grit and glory surrounding pirates and privateers, the reality was often a far more brutal existence. Life aboard these ships was harsh – cramped quarters, poor food provisions, rampant disease, and the constant threat of violent death or severe injury. Despite this grim reality, many sailors willingly chose this life to escape poverty, seek fame amongst the criminal underworld or simply gain a sliver of freedom amidst an otherwise bleak existence.

Over time though, as colonial powers established stronger navies and more secure trade routes within their territories, piracy began facing relentless opposition. Gradually pressured from all sides by more disciplined navies employing heavier firepower and swifter vessels, it seemed pirates had reached their zenith. Official pardons offered by governments further diminished pirate ranks with many opting for clemency over continued resistance.

Conversely, the practice of privateering diminished with the advent of more formalized rules governing international commerce and warfare during the latter half of the 18th century onwards. The United States Congress would officially denounce the issuing of letters of marque in 1856. Privateers were ultimately replaced by regular state navies, marking the end of an era.

While the era of pirates and privateers may have been consigned to the annals of history, they continue to hold a unique and enduring fascination worldwide. These guardians of their age captured the imagination through their daring exploits, unbreakable spirit, and defiance against an unforgiving world. Their fierce drive for freedom and retribution against the establishment continues to resonate today, making them an essential part of military history.

Early Modern Period Militaries in Asia and Africa

Overview of Influential Militaristic States

The Early Modern Period was defined by the establishment of powerful empires, marked by their vast territories, economic wealth, and enduring cultural and political legacies. Among the most influential of these were the Maratha Empire in India, the Mughal Empire, which spanned much of present-day India, Pakistan, and Bangladesh; the Safavid Dynasty in Persia (modern-day Iran), and several great African kingdoms. Each of these states possessed remarkable military prowess that contributed to their prosperity and territorial expansion.

1. The Maratha Empire (1674-1818): The Marathas were a formidable force in India from the late 17th to early 19th centuries. Founded by Shivaji Bhonsle, a renowned guerrilla warrior and national hero, the Maratha Empire was known for its unparalleled tactics in warfare and strategic diplomacy. At its peak, it covered a significant portion of India, surpassing the size of European kingdoms during that era.

Marathas practiced guerrilla warfare by exploiting their knowledge of local terrain to expertly defend against invaders. Their ability to move swiftly through mountainous regions and attack enemies using surprise and ambush contributed to their prowess in battle. The rugged region of Deccan Plateau also enabled them to build impregnable forts.

The fall of the Maratha Empire came with their defeat at the hands of the British East India Company during the Anglo-Maratha Wars (1775-1818), ending one of India's most powerful militaristic states.

2. The Mughal Empire (1526-1858): The Mughals originated in Central Asia and established a vast empire spanning modern-day India, Pakistan, Bangladesh, and Afghanistan. Under great rulers like Babur, Akbar the Great, and Shah Jahan, the Mughal Empire became synonymous with remarkable military power, architectural splendor, and cultural achievements.

One key factor behind Mughal success was their adept use of gunpowder weaponry, such as cannons and firearms. They also adopted siege tactics and cavalry maneuvers that were unparalleled at the time. Their fortresses and architectural achievements, like the Red Fort and Taj Mahal, reflected the empire's opulence and military might.

The decline of the Mughal Empire transpired over several centuries due to multiple factors, including weak emperors and internal strife. Their eventual collapse came in 1858 when the British Crown formally took control of India.

3. The Safavid Empire (1501-1736): The Safavids were a Shiite Muslim dynasty that ruled Persia (now Iran) in the 16th century. They are credited with uniting various Persian territories under a single empire through their military strength and firm religious beliefs.

The Safavid military was known for its elite corps of fighters called Qizilbash, who gained a fierce reputation on the battlefield for their bravery and combat expertise. They also embraced innovative tactics such as using matchlock muskets, which allowed them to gain an edge over their enemies.

Internal power struggles, combined with external threats from neighboring empires like the Ottomans, led to the decline of this once-mighty Persian empire.

4. African Kingdoms: In ancient Africa, numerous kingdoms rose to prominence such as Mali in West Africa (1235-1540), Kongo in

Central Africa (1390-1857), and Zulu in Southern Africa (1816-1897).

Mali is renowned for its powerful kings like Mansa Musa who expanded its territory and boosted trade on a vast level. Mali's wealth in gold contributed to its economic influence while its military prowess allowed it to conquer neighboring kingdoms.

The Kingdom of Kongo was another militarily strong state with intricate local alliances maintaining its expansive territory. The Kongo warriors excelled at using bows, knives, and spears in battle.

Lastly, the Zulu Kingdom proved its military acumen under the formidable leadership of King Shaka Zulu, who modernized warfare strategies. The Zulu army transformed from a militia into a disciplined force through innovative tactics and weapons, leading to numerous victories in Southern Africa.

Military Technologies and Strategic Innovations

The early modern period, spanning roughly from the 15th to the 18th century, witnessed significant developments and innovations in the military technology and strategy, particularly within Asian and African states. These advances played a substantial role in shaping the trajectory of global history and contributed towards the rise of powerful empires.

In Asia, one of the most notable military advancements was the introduction of gunpowder weapons. Although gunpowder itself originated in China around the 9th century, it was during the early modern period that it gained widespread use across Asia. Firearms like muskets, arquebuses, and cannons revolutionized warfare, making armored knights obsolete and giving rise to new tactics built around massed infantry formations supported by artillery.

One example of such tactical innovation was the famous "turtle ship" employed by Admiral Yi Sun-sin during his defense of Korea against a numerically superior Japanese invasion force in 1592. This heavily armed naval vessel featured a spiked roof to deter Japanese boarding attempts while its arsenal of cannons allowed it to decimate enemy fleets with ease. The turtle ship's innovative design played a pivotal role in Korean naval victories, helping secure Korea's independence.

Another impactful military innovation in Asia during this period was the extensive use of elephant-mounted troops in southeast Asian warfare. While elephants had been employed across Asia for centuries, such tactics reached their zenith during the rise of Siam (now Thailand) under King Naresuan in the late 16th century. In one famous battle, Naresuan rode an elephant into combat against Burmese forces led by Mingyi Swa, eventually challenging him to single combat which resulted in Swa's death.

The early modern period also witnessed significant military advances within Africa. The emergence of powerful centralized states enabled kingdoms like Ethiopia and Kongo to maintain large standing armies capable of tackling external threats and policing internal dissent. It was during this era that some of Africa's most ambitious military campaigns and ambitious wars were executed— in particular, the Ethiopian campaigns led by Emperor Tewodros II and Menelik II stand out as notable examples.

Amongst the numerous technological advancements in the African theatre, one particularly impactful development was the incorporation of Portuguese firearms. In the late 15th century, Kongo became one of Africa's first kingdoms to employ firearms at scale. Such adoption was possible due to diplomatic relationships it forged with Portugal, which ensured access to these weapons that heavily tipped combat in favor of their users. These firearms would later play a significant role in redefining warfare across West Africa as well.

In addition to technological innovations, African militaries also began implementing novel strategies to maximize their efficiency on the battlefield. One such example can be seen in Ethiopia's frequent use of dense terrain and deceptive tactics to neutralize more sophisticated enemies. During the Battle of Adwa in 1896, under the command of Menelik II, Ethiopian forces employed these strategic ploys against an Italian colonial force who, despite their advanced weaponry and training, succumbed largely due to their unfamiliarity with guerrilla warfare.

While European militaries occupied much historical focus from this period onwards, it is essential not to overlook the monumental impact Asian and African forces had on shaping global military history by taking advantage of advanced tactics and technology. The innovative strategies utilized during infamous battles like Korea's naval victory against Japan or Ethiopia's legendary defeat of Italy are prime examples.

The early modern period's Asian and African forces demonstrated incredible adaptability and innovation as they confronted new challenges on the battlefield. These technological leaps enabled previously vulnerable states to defend themselves against hostile neighbors or assert their dominance within wider regions.

Influence of European Powers on Shaping their Military

As Europeans began exploring new territories and expanding their empires, the need for efficient weapon systems and strategies arose. The influence of European powers on shaping their military forces in Asia and Africa during this period significantly contributed to the development and prowess of some of the most powerful militaries in history.

One major factor in this transformation was the adoption of European military technology. Gunpowder weaponry, such as cannons and muskets, were first introduced to Asia through European traders and played a pivotal role in drastically changing local warfare methods. Not only did this new form of artillery give an immense advantage to the forces that employed them, but it also allowed for new tactics that favored stand-and-fight strategies over traditional mobile warfare. In response to these advancements, Asian militaries incorporated these weapons into their own arsenals, developing unique tactics and strategies around them.

In Africa, European contact directly influenced how leaders formed their military units. West African states like Dahomey were heavily impacted by European demand for slaves. As a result, Dahomey built up its army to capture more slaves from its neighbors by adopting European firearms into their tactics. This centralized power eventually led to the formation of elite military units like the Ahosi or "Dahomey Amazons," composed solely of female warriors trained in both hand-to-hand combat and firearms usage.

Similarly, the Ottoman Empire experienced significant development as it embraced European military technology. Recognizing its importance, Ottoman leaders sought alliances with skilled specialists who could help refine their existing arsenals and train soldiers in modern techniques. Janissaries—elite infantrymen part of the larger Sipahi class—were one such product of these efforts, proving their prowess in various campaigns against traditional powers in Europe and Asia.

Besides technology, the influence of European military strategies on Asian and African armies was also critical in shaping their development. The Portuguese Empire established a global maritime empire in the early 16th century, reaching India, East Asia, and West Africa. Their expansionist tactics paved the way for other European powers to follow. Maritime exploration allowed these nations to establish superior supply lines and create efficient communication systems on sea routes.

The Dutch East India Company notably implemented a military strategy using a mix of commerce and colonization to control key trading areas within Asia. Their paramilitary approach—protecting their interests with formidable private armies—demonstrated how

European forces could quickly transform politics and economies of regions around the world.

In Africa, European influence drastically impacted local military systems as well. Kingdoms within the geographic region found it increasingly necessary to trade for modern weapons and engage with wider networks—both for external defenses against European threats and internal power struggles amongst rivals. Larger states like the Oyo Empire of Nigeria had highly organized and centralized military institutions that showcased European influence through adapted weaponry and tactics.

Despite the significant changes brought by European interaction, many Asian and African militaries during this period continued valuing traditional practices alongside modern advancements. The Japanese samurai, for example, still held immense political power throughout society despite newly introduced firearms from European traders. Similarly, Africa's Zulu warriors maintained sophisticated battle strategies despite a lack of advanced weaponry—an obstacle they would continue facing in future conflicts with colonial forces.

Latin American Revolutionary Wars & Independence Movements

Examination of Key Military Forces

The 19th century marked a period of revolutionary struggle and social upheavals, which ultimately established the modern-day political landscape of Latin America. Various independent movements were sparked during this period, leading to the creation of republics and democracies across the Americas.

1. The Argentine War for Independence (1810-1816): At the turn of the century, Argentina was gripped by a battle for independence against Spanish rule led by Marshal José de San Martín. San Martín's strategic genius enabled him to defy Spanish strongholds, unite disparate military forces, and secure Argentina's sovereignty. His stalwart Army of the Andes traversed treacherous mountains, conditions, and terrain to crush Spanish forces occupying nearby states. In an exceptional display of military prowess, San Martín defeated royalist troops at Chacabuco in 1817 and Maipú in 1818, securing Chile's independence as well.

2. The Wars for Independence (1810-1824): Eager to replicate Argentina's newfound autonomy, various countries followed suit as they advanced toward liberation. Simón Bolívar emerged as the central figure in these wars, spearheading freedom movements across Colombia (also known as New Granada), Venezuela, Ecuador, Peru, and Bolivia.

Leading an army predominantly comprised of Creoles, Bolívar made his mark through smart tactics and inspiring leadership. Though his forces were numerically inferior compared to Spanish might in many instances—such as at Boyacá in Colombia and

Carabobo in Venezuela—Bolívar persevered to win decisive battles using surprise assaults and swifter movements.

3. The Brazilian War of Independence (1821-1825): Unlike other Latin American uprisings predominantly led by military commanders, the Brazilian war effort was distinguished by its monarchic beginnings. When its king, João VI, return to Portugal in 1821, Brazil was declared a separate kingdom under the command of his son, Dom Pedro. The prince's pro-independence stance gained traction and culminated in Brazil's independence on September 7th, 1822.

Despite open conflict with Portugal over territorial claims, Brazil's war for independence was far less bloody and volatile than her neighbors'. Under José Bonifácio de Andrada e Silva's guidance as Pedro's Minister, a modest army comprising Brazilian-born officers and units—such as the Volunteers of the Prince and the Imperial Guard—encouraged Brazil's progression toward independence.

4. The Mexican War of Independence (1810-1821): Pushed to the brink by political, societal, and economic strife within colonial Mexico, reformists sought change. This ignited the desire for independence from Spain and fueled several factions rallying for warfare: Insurgents who endeavored to seize territory from Spanish authorities; royalists who sought to protect Spanish power; and Creole elites conflicted between both camps.

This tense atmosphere reached a boiling point on September 16th, 1810, when Miguel Hidalgo y Costilla gave his impassioned Grito de Dolores speech. This galvanized widespread support for Mexican independence; marquee military leaders endorse the effort—most notably Ignacio Allende and José María Morelos.

The quest for a fully independent Mexico saw significant moments such as guerrilla tactics employed by Guadalupe Victoria, alongside decisive battles led by Agustín de Iturbide who declared independence in Plan de Iguala (1821). Ultimately, these consolidated efforts enabled an independent but monarchical Mexico.

Emphasis on Prominent Leaders

Simón Bolívar and José de San Martín are remarkable generals from South America led their forces to victory against oppressive colonial regimes in the 1800s, paving the way for a new era of independence and self-determination in Latin America. Their accomplishments would become legendary, earning them a place among the top 100 greatest military leaders throughout history.

Simón Bolívar, known as El Libertador, was born in Caracas, Venezuela, in 1783. Raised within an elite family of the colonial Venezuelan society, he received an education that exposed him to the ideas of Enlightenment philosophers such as Rousseau and Montesquieu. Profoundly influenced by their writings on democracy and social equality, Bolívar swore to liberate his people from Spanish rule and dedicated his life to achieving this feat.

Bolívar's military campaigns spanned an astonishingly vast area from present-day Venezuela to Bolivia, Colombia, Ecuador, and Peru. Under his charismatic leadership and strategic genius, Bolívar united the people of these territories who would eventually form the specter of 'Gran Colombia.' His most famous battle came at Boyacá in 1819 when his forces ingeniously crossed the Andes Mountain to surprise their enemies in a decisive victory.

However, despite his many triumphs on the battlefield and his staunch commitment to emancipation from colonial oppression, Bolívar failed in creating stability in newfound republics. Yet today, regions like Colombia reverently carry Simón Bolívar's name with pride – testament to the impact this exceptional leader had on South American history.

José de San Martín was born in Argentina in 1778 before relocating with his family to Spain when he was just a child. In an incredible twist of fate, San Martín's military career would begin fighting for their colonial masters in both Spain and Portugal. San Martín distinguished himself in multiple battles against the French during the Peninsular War, proving his worth with great martial skill and prowess.

As the Enlightenment ideas simmered among Spanish colonies, San Martín had his ideological transformation – deciding to devote his life to liberating the Spanish-speaking regions of South America from imperial rule. With strong convictions, he returned to his native Argentina in 1812.

San Martín first set off to liberate Argentina before turning his attention towards Chile and Peru. One of his most impressive feats was leading a daring army across the towering Andes in an audacious bid to outflank the Spanish. This gamble ultimately paid off – resulting in several vital victories at Chacabuco and Maipú, which led to Chile's liberation.

In 1821, San Martín's forces entered Lima – unopposed. Later that year, he declared Peruvian independence from Spain and earned one final title: "Protector of Peru." However, in a move that displayed humility and dedication to Latin American unity, San Martín yielded power to Bolívar amidst concerns over clashing ambitions in order to avoid potential civil war.

In a poignant meeting between these two visionaries at Guayaquil in 1822, a glance into both their perseverance against overwhelming odds was evident. This encounter underscored the historic impact these two exceptional leaders had on South American history.

Bolívar's leadership across an unimaginable expanse of territories earned him the respect and esteem of generations to come. Similarly, José de San Martín's selfless devotion to others' freedom leaves him etched as a true embodiment of valor and magnanimity.

These iconic leaders – Simón Bolívar and José de San Martín – will always remain as beacons of inspiration throughout military history.

Their commitment to the ideals of liberty, unity, and self-sacrifice undoubtedly earned them a place in our hearts and memory as a testament to the power of strategic vision and human resilience.

Analysis of Guerilla Tactics in Latin American Conflicts

One of the seminal Latin American conflicts involving guerrilla warfare was the Cuban Revolution (1953-1959). Under the leadership of Fidel Castro and Che Guevara, a small group of revolutionaries, known as "guerrilleros," managed to overthrow the US-backed dictator Fulgencio Batista. The success of this revolution can be attributed to various guerrilla tactics, such as blending with the local population, utilizing the terrain effectively and avoiding direct confrontation with government forces.

In the dense forested areas, Cuban guerrillas were able to build their base camps, train, and mobilize their forces efficiently. They survived on limited resources by adapting to their environment and treating the local communities with respect, thereby gaining their trust and support.

The Sandinista movement in Nicaragua (1961-1979) is another critical example of successful guerrilla warfare in Latin America. Named after Augusto César Sandino, who resisted US military occupation in the 1920s-1930s, this movement aimed to topple the US-backed Somoza dictatorship. Sandinistas leveraged similar guerrilla tactics as Cuban revolutionaries. They struck at night when government troops were less prepared and established ambush points on known routes used by government forces.

In sharp contrast to these successful cases is Colombia's Revolutionary Armed Forces of Colombia (FARC), which spent more than five decades fighting against the Colombian government. Throughout its existence, FARC employed ambushes, kidnapping for ransom, and bombings against both military targets and civilian infrastructure. The group utilized drug trafficking money to fund its operations and gain influence in rural areas.

However, Colombia's terrain and FARC's tactics created a long-lasting stalemate rather than significant political change. Although the Cuban Revolution and the Sandinista movement utilized drug trafficking as well, their primary goal was political and social change. The FARC's monetary affiliation with drug trafficking potentially obscured its ideological aims, stretching its armed struggle for several decades without achieving tangible results.

The Zapatistas rebellion in Mexico (1994-present) is yet another instance of a guerrilla movement seeking radical change in Latin America. The Zapatista National Liberation Army (EZLN) relied on public support and used less violent tactics than their counterparts in Nicaragua or Cuba. Their strategy focused on occupying key villages and towns, avoiding direct confrontations with government forces. Ultimately, their main battle has been for media attention and public opinion rather than military conquests. Unfortunately, the Mexican government responded with aggressive military force, making it challenging for the EZLN to accomplish most of their goals.

The analysis of guerrilla tactics in Latin American conflicts reveals patterns that have defined their successes or failures:

1. **A strong local support base**: Movements with significant local backing increased their chances of success. For instance, the Cuban Revolution was marked by a good relationship between guerrillas and rural communities.
2. **Effective use of terrain:** Guerrillas adeptly exploited natural environments that favored asymmetrical warfare, such as dense forests and swamplands as hideouts and ambush points.
3. **Clarity of ideology:** Successful movements focused on concrete political objectives that rallied popular sentiment.

4. **Adaptability:** Successful guerrilla groups were able to evolve their strategies suited to different situations without compromising the broader objectives.

19th Century Imperialism & Colonization

The Role of Major Imperial Powers' Militaries

During the 19th century, the world experienced significant changes in geopolitics as major imperial powers expanded their territories and influence across the globe. The militaries of these nations played a crucial role in extending their political power and control, transforming the strategic landscape throughout this period.

The British Empire reached its zenith under Queen Victoria (1837-1901), emerging as one of the most dominant forces in the world. The Royal Navy ensured Britain's maritime supremacy, projecting its influence across various continents while protecting vital trade routes. British naval innovations pioneered during this era – such as ironclad ships and advancements in naval artillery – played a significant role in solidifying its dominance over the seas.

Moreover, the British Army demonstrated considerable presence across colonies worldwide, employing both European officers and local troops. Through a combination of direct military conquests and diplomatic alliances with local rulers, Britain established hegemony over India, South Africa, Australia, and Canada. The British Indian Army emerged as an essential tool for administering imperial rule within the region; it helped suppress various uprisings like the Indian Rebellion of 1857 while contributing to Britain's warfare elsewhere.

In parallel with Britain's global ascendency, France remained a prominent player on both European and international levels throughout the 19th century under Napoleon III (1852-1870). The French Army underwent significant reforms under his reign, embracing new technology and training techniques that would ensure its ability to project power on an international scale. These developments contributed to French success in conflicts like the Crimean War (1853-1856) and furthered its colonial pursuits across regions like Southeast Asia and North Africa.

However, France experienced a bitter defeat in the Franco-Prussian War (1870-1871), a turning point that marked the rise of German military power. This development initiated by Otto von Bismarck saw the unification of German states under Prussia's leadership, bringing about a new global player in the form of the German Empire. The German Army underwent rapid modernization, adopting contemporary strategic thinking such as the Schlieffen Plan, flanked by innovative arms production techniques.

The prowess of Germany's armed forces placed a new challenge for other European powers to contend with, fueling what would become an escalating arms race throughout the late 19th century. The outcome of the Franco-Prussian War shifted power dynamics across Europe and laid the groundwork for considerable military and geopolitical tensions that set the stage for World War I.

Another significant player during this time, Russia held ambitions of strengthening its presence globally by reinforcing its strategic position upon Eastern Europe and Central Asia. The Russian Army – although disciplined and powerful – faced limitations like outdated weaponry and insufficient logistics capabilities, restricting their ability to project power beyond their immediate sphere of influence. The Russo-Japanese War (1904-1905) marked a moment of reckoning for Russia's military power, demonstrating an inability to match foes on equal footing technologically and ultimately resulting in defeat.

The 19th century marked a tumultuous era in which major imperial powers used their militaries to extend their global influence, clash with rivals, and defend their territorial interests. These developments dramatically altered power dynamics worldwide, and it became apparent that modern technology – from steam-powered warships to new artillery strategies – played an essential role in determining a nation's ability to assert itself on the global stage.

As these military systems evolved throughout this period of history, they laid down the foundations upon which future military developments would arise well into the 20th century. In addition, rivalries between imperial powers resulted in dramatic shifts across political landscapes, directly influencing the unfolding of our modern world today.

Colonial Wars and Resistance Movements

The 19th century was a period that witnessed the rapid expansion of colonial powers, particularly those of the British Empire, French Empire, and other European nations. These colonial empires sought control over the resources, markets, and strategic territories in regions such as Africa, Asia, and the Pacific. This era was marked by struggles between colonized populations and their colonizers, as well as resistance movements that fought for independence and self-determination.

1. The Opium Wars (1839-1842; 1856-1860): The Opium Wars were the result of British demands for unrestricted opium trade with China. Resisting British encroachments on its sovereignty led China to prohibit opium importation and destroy vast quantities of seized contraband. Subsequently, Britain launched expeditions to force China into submission, underlining the unequal relationship between Western colonial powers and non-European nations. The aftermath saw China ceding territories to Britain along with other concessions.

2. First Anglo-Afghan War (1839-1842): The Great Game - the geopolitical contest between Russia and Britain in Central Asia - led to Britain's invasion of Afghanistan in 1839. This was an attempt to extend British influence, counter a Russian advance, and ensure a pro-British Afghan ruler in power. Initially successful, the British eventually faced rebellion from Afghans under Sher Ali Khan and his son Akbar Khan. A devastating retreat from Kabul in January 1842 saw heavy losses for the British forces; however, they did capture Kabul later that September before withdrawing from Afghanistan altogether.

3. Indian Rebellion of 1857: The Indian Rebellion was a widespread uprising against British rule originating from resentment over various issues encompassing economic exploitation, social injustices, and religious imperialism. Although unsuccessful, the revolt had far-reaching consequences for Indian and British history. It led to the dissolution of the British East India Company and a consolidation of colonial administration under direct control of the British Crown.

4. French Conquest of Algeria (1830-1847): In 1830, France invaded Algeria under the pretext of offsetting an unsettled debt. The war that followed pitted native resistance movements led by the likes of Emir Abdelkader against French military might. After years of guerrilla warfare, Abdelkader finally surrendered in 1847. Nonetheless, French rule continued to face stiff resistance due to its exploitative policies and insensitivity towards Algerian culture and religion.

5. Mahdist War (1881–1899): In response to Egyptian rule in Sudan and British expansionism in Africa, a large-scale rebellion erupted in Sudan led by Muhammad Ahmad bin Abd Allah, a religious leader claiming to be the mahdi - a messianic redeemer figure in Islamic belief. The movement quickly gained momentum due to rampant fervor among oppressed populations longing for spiritual redemption and social justice. After many skirmishes and prolonged resistance, Anglo-Egyptian forces ultimately defeated struggling remnants of the Mahdist forces in 1899.

6. Xhosa Wars (1779–1879: These series of wars between European settlers and indigenous Xhosa tribes in southern Africa further highlighted imperial encroachment on native lands throughout the 19th century. While initially sparked by disputes over grazing lands on territory borders, these conflicts grew into large-scale clashes between colonizers and indigenous populations opposing colonization efforts imposed upon them.

7. New Zealand Wars (1845-1872): The New Zealand Wars between Maori tribes and British settlers were driven by disagreements regarding land rights and sovereignty after the signing of the Treaty of Waitangi in 1840. Over time, these skirmishes grew into protracted engagements, culminating in multiple armed conflicts across the country. Eventually, British forces emerged victorious but not without a long-lasting impact on the relationship between Maori and Europeans in New Zealand.

Impact On Global Military Landscape

The 19th century was a pivotal era in the evolution of military power and the world, driven by imperialism and colonization. The seized territories of distant lands led to intense competition among European powers, significantly shaping their military strategies and global influence.

The "Scramble for Africa" in the early 1870s is perhaps the epitome of this period, when countries like England, Germany, France, Belgium, Italy, Portugal, and Spain vied for control over African territories. Apart from Africa, Southeast Asia and the Pacific got embroiled in this frenzy as well. This chapter delves into the implications of imperialism and colonization on the world's military landscape during this transformative period.

One key impact of imperialism was the rapid expansion of military forces. Countries scrambled to build stronger armies and navies by modernizing weaponry and improving supply lines. This expansion was essential to maintain control over lucrative colonies while deterring encroachment by rival powers.

Technological advancements played a crucial role as well. The Industrial Revolution facilitated the mass production of firearms, ammunition, and other armaments that bolstered military prowess. Inventive machines like Hiram Maxim's automatic machine gun made their debut on battlefields. Armor plating for ships transformed naval warfare – wooden battleships were gradually replaced by robust iron-clad ships.

Moreover, new strategies evolved due to these advancements – warfare tactics developed beyond conventional confrontations with guerilla warfare becoming more prominent. The Boer War that raged between 1899 and 1902 in South Africa is a prime example of how European imperial forces adapted guerilla tactics against their local adversaries.

Colonization also fueled extensive military expeditions – superior weaponry gave colonizers an advantage to consolidate territories they sought after. If diplomacy failed to bring indigenous rulers under their command, militaries were employed to quell resistance forcefully. These conquests led to an entrenched military presence across the globe, with permanent garrisons stationed in strategic outposts.

Imperial powers also relied heavily on local armed forces. Many colonized societies were required to supply manpower for their occupiers, often fighting under their banners. These indigenous soldiers, complemented by European officers, became an integral part of many imperial armies. In some instances, these local forces transitioned into national armies upon achieving independence from colonization.

Divisive tactics imposed upon native populations to maintain control also affected the military landscape during this epoch. "Divide and rule" as a strategy compelled certain ethnicities within colonies to play off against others. This strife often resulted in bolstering military infrastructures that sought to suppress dissent. At times, these strategies came at the cost of heavy casualties or even genocide.

The colonization of diverse regions introduced the European powers to several indigenous military technologies and skills adapted from local terrains. These skills included enhanced marksmanship in forests, advanced use of primitive weaponry, and bolstered ambush and guerilla tactics. Several European powers incorporated these skills into their own military doctrines, improving their overall effectiveness on both foreign and domestic battlegrounds.

The imperial ambitions ignited fierce rivalries among major European powers, culminating in a series of wars like the Russo-Japanese War (1904-1905) and ultimately led to World War I (1914-1918). The arms race associated with colonial expansion fueled tensions that marked the dawn of this global conflict. In fact, World War I's origins can be traced back to colonial disputes over territory and resources.

Militaries in the Age of World War I

Analysis of Influential Militaries in World War I

World War I, also known as the Great War, took place between 1914 and 1918 and involved many nations of the world. The war saw the rise and influence of powerful militaries such as the Entente Powers, including the British Empire, France, and Russia, and the Central Powers consisting of Germany, Austria-Hungary, and the Ottoman Empire.

Entente Powers

The Entente Powers were a coalition of countries that opposed the Central Powers during World War I. The three primary members were France, Russia, and the United Kingdom, and they were later joined by several other nations, including Italy and the United States.

1. **France:** The French military played a crucial role in World War I due to their strategic location and well-trained army. They suffered massive casualties throughout the conflict but consistently displayed unwavering determination. Their most significant contributions came from deploying highly disciplined infantry divisions, creating elaborate trenches systems, and utilizing cutting-edge weaponry like the 75mm field gun.
2. **Russia:** The Russian Empire was one of the largest combatants during World War I. The vastness of its territory provided ample resources for waging war, but its military was plagued by internal issues such as archaic tactics and inadequate leadership. Regardless, Russian forces managed to launch successful offensives against Austria-Hungary and Germany, notably at Galicia and Brusilov Offensive.

3. **United Kingdom:** Among Entente militaries, Britain stood out for its naval dominance and technological prowess. The Royal Navy's supremacy played an essential part in controlling sea lanes for strategic purposes, ensuring resources could be transported easily from across their empire. Additionally, British innovations such as tanks and aircraft proved instrumental in gaining an edge against enemy forces on land.

4. **Italy:** Although initially part of Central Powers through the Triple Alliance with Germany and Austria-Hungary, Italy declared neutrality in 1914 and joined the Entente Powers the following year. This switch proved vital as Italy's Alpine Warfare skills occupied Austrian troops, diverting them from the Eastern Front.

5. **United States:** The late entry of the United States into World War I significantly impacted the conflict's outcome. The American Expeditionary Force played a pivotal role in tipping the scales in favor of the Entente Powers, and the surge of resources and manpower they provided were invaluable.

Central Powers

At the outbreak of World War I, the Central Powers initially consisted of Germany, Austria-Hungary, and Italy. However, with Italy eventually defecting to join the Entente Powers, the alliance was forced to restructure. They were later joined by Ottoman Empire and Bulgaria.

1. **Germany:** Boasting one of Europe's most powerful military machines, Germany was instrumental in shaping World War I's tactics and strategies. Their efficient logistical networks allowed for rapid troop movement, exemplified in the Schlieffen Plan. On several occasions, Germany displayed their military prowess by pushing back enemy forces and gaining ground.

2. **Austria-Hungary:** This highly diverse empire encompassed various nations within its borders, leading to challenges in standardizing their military forces. While their soldiers were

well-trained and equipped with modern artillery at the war's onset, strategic missteps and setbacks eroded their effectiveness over time. Nevertheless, Austria-Hungary played a significant role in both Eastern and Italian Fronts throughout the conflict.

3. **Ottoman Empire:** Engaged on multiple fronts during World War I, this once-mighty empire found itself weakening due to internal strife and territorial losses. Despite this decline, the Ottoman military managed to inflict significant damage on Entente forces across several key battles such as Gallipoli and Kut al-Amara.

4. **Bulgaria:** Though not as powerful as Germany or Austria-Hungary, Bulgaria surprisingly became an essential asset for the Central Powers. Their army was particularly effective in the Southern Front against Serbia and Romania, and they managed to gain valuable territories throughout the war.

Trench Warfare Tactics and Technological Advancements

The outbreak of the Great War forced armies to adapt to modern mechanized combat quickly. With both sides equipped with swift-firing machine guns, direct assaults left soldiers exposed and vulnerable. As battles dragged on with no clear victor, both sides dug in – literally – seeking cover from enemy fire amidst vast networks of trenches.

Trenches stretched over 400 miles from North Sea to Switzerland's border, carving through France like an ugly scar. Soldiers lived and fought under grim conditions, facing diseases, harsh weather, extreme confinement, and constant threat of artillery bombardments or gas attacks.

To navigate this frozen battlefield landscape effectively required various tactics. Raiding parties often ventured into enemy territory under cover of darkness for reconnaissance or to sabotage enemy outposts. These small surprise attack were designed to weaken enemy defenses while gaining valuable intelligence.

To exploit any weaknesses found during such raids, commanders relied upon massive infantry offensives. Soldiers would "go over the top" by climbing out of their trenches and charge through rain-drenched mud towards enemy lines. Artillery barrages would precede these attacks to soften opponents' defenses and cover infantry advances. Unfortunately for attackers, many attempts to utilize this tactic ended in excessive casualties due to machine gun fire from well-prepared defenders.

One of the most feared innovations during World War I was poison gas usage. Its introduction transformed warfare as adversaries struggled with new countermeasures vital for survival. Initially utilized by Germany at Ypres in 1915, chlorine gas bellowed through trenches like a toxic fog, causing terrifying lung damage, choking, and slow suffocation.

Armies quickly developed defenses against gas attacks, adopting gas masks and special clothing. In response, more potent gases, such as phosgene and mustard gas, were added to both sides' deadly arsenals. Though the introduction of poisonous gases contributed to the war's human cost and terror, it also served as a powerful driver for military research into chemical defense - which would have repercussions far beyond the battlefield.

As the war stagnated, the need for armored fighting vehicles became apparent: vehicles capable of crossing trenches and shielding soldiers from enemy fire. The first tanks were introduced in 1916 on the British side. These lumbering steel fortresses evoked awe and terror across enemy lines. Despite their limitations - slow speed and vulnerability to mechanical failure - tanks heralded a seismic shift in warfare.

Another significant leap forward came with aerial combat. During World War I, aircraft commanded considerable strategic importance despite their crude simplicity by modern standards. Equipped primarily for reconnaissance missions at first, fighter planes took to the skies in an effort to undermine their opponents' intelligence operations.

The introduction of machine guns on planes gave impetus to aerial warfare where nimble pilots became known as aces who engaged each other in thrilling dogfights above battlefields. To supplement these engagements, zeppelins and lighter-than-air craft served as bombing platforms over enemy territories.

To maintain communications during tumultuous combat in the trenches, dedicated telephone lines were set up between outposts and headquarters. The use of semaphores and lanterns allowed for transmission of coded messages during nighttime operations. Developing complex codes ensured that intercepted messages could not be read by enemy intelligence services.

The landscape of trench warfare shifted as new tactics were adopted and fresh technologies surfaced during World War I. Bombardments, assaults "over the top," horrors of gas attacks, advent of tanks paving way for mechanized warfare - all contributed to the spirit of innovation and the determination to overcome harrowing conditions. The brutality and ingenuity of trench warfare stands as a grisly testament to the devastating human cost and unrelenting drive for victory woven throughout military history.

Social, Economic, and Political Effects

The Great War reshaped the world in more ways than one. It wasn't just a military conflict; it had far-reaching social, economic, and political effects on societies across the globe. Some of these impacts have permanently changed the course of human history.

Social Effects

The war caused immense suffering and loss for millions. From 1914 to 1918, people on both sides of the conflict saw their lives transformed in different ways. For those in the warring countries, day-to-day life was marked by food shortages, conscription, harsh workplace conditions, and fear for their loved ones fighting at the front.

Traditional gender roles were altered as women stepped up to fill positions left vacant by men going off to fight. With women taking active roles in industry and agriculture sectors while remaining pillars of support for their families back home, they contributed greatly to the war effort. Their newfound importance led to an evolution in how women were seen and treated in society; suffrage movements gained momentum after the war as a result.

World War I also led to huge displacement of populations. People fled from their homes and towns as refugee crises added to the toll of lives lost during battles. Countries came face-to-face with cultural clashes as well as newfound empathy for those caught up in the global chaos.

Economic Effects

The war brought devastating economic consequences for all involved. The belligerent countries spent vast sums of money to finance their military efforts; by financing through loans and selling bonds to citizens and foreign entities alike increased national debts exponentially.

Once the war ended, European economies faced major challenges in rebuilding infrastructure shattered by years of conflict. Not only did such tasks require enormous funds; they also demanded time and labor to bring about recovery.

In Germany alone, post-war economic hardship was crushing. The punitive terms outlined in the Treaty of Versailles subjected the German people to massive inflation, widespread poverty and unemployment. The dire economic state opened doors for extremist ideologies, setting the stage for Adolf Hitler's rise to power.

On the other hand, while Europe burned, America prospered. American industries boomed due to European markets eager for war supplies and as countries began rebuilding efforts after hostilities ceased. The United States emerged from World War I as an economic superpower.

Political Effects

The war created rippling political changes across Europe and inspired colonies around the world to clamor for self-determination. Four major empires – the Ottoman, Austro-Hungarian, Russian, and German – fell apart in the aftermath of World War I. As a result, numerous new nations were born out of old borders. The Treaty of Versailles redrew map lines and created fledgling democracies in regions that had once been ruled by monarchs.

In Russia, political unrest escalated into a full-fledged revolution culminating with removal of Tsar Nicholas II from power and eventual establishment of a communist regime under Lenin's leadership. This profound shift set Russia on a collision course with capitalist Western countries during the forthcoming Cold War.

Colonial countries in Africa and Asia witnessed their governing imperial powers weakened by the strains of war. Emboldened by whispers of freedom promised in Wilson's Fourteen Points, independence movements gained momentum across colonized nations worldwide.

Militaries in the Age of World War II

Assessment of Influential Militaries in World War II

World War II, a global conflict that lasted from 1939 to 1945, was one of the most pivotal and transformative periods in human history. It involved the majority of the world's nations, including all the great powers, split into two opposing military alliances: the Allies and the Axis Powers.

The Allies: United States, Soviet Union, and Great Britain

The United States entered the war after being attacked at Pearl Harbor in December 1941. It quickly ramped up its military production, igniting an economic boom that aided its allies. The US mobilized its vast resources to build a powerful army that excelled in air, land, and sea warfare. Its most influential role was in aerial attacks on enemy infrastructure and supplying crucial resources and support to its Allies.

The Soviet Union's Red Army was crucial in defeating Nazi Germany on the Eastern Front. Despite facing horrendous casualties and early setbacks, they displayed an unrelenting will to fight and made Hitler pay a high price for his invasion. The Red Army became well-known for their fierce endurance and unfaltering spirit under extreme conditions. Key battles such as Stalingrad demonstrated their strength in urban warfare and tenacity when faced with insurmountable odds.

Great Britain stood as an important bulwark against Nazi aggression, with a legendary resilience led by Prime Minister Winston Churchill. The Royal Air Force's role in defeating the Luftwaffe during the Battle of Britain was pivotal to preventing an

Axis invasion of their homeland. British intelligence also provided essential information that ultimately helped turn the tide of war through espionage and code breaking.

The Axis Powers: Germany, Italy, and Japan

Nazi Germany's military might was truly formidable during World War II. Armed with advanced technology and precise strategies helmed by notable commanders such as Erwin Rommel and Heinz Guderian, the Blitzkrieg tactics brought a swift defeat to many European nations. The elite Waffen SS units and gargantuan Tiger tanks were fierce adversaries on the battlefield. However, Hitler's tendency to interfere with military decisions ultimately contributed to their downfall.

Italy's military, led by Fascist dictator Benito Mussolini, saw early successes in North Africa and the Balkans. Although markedly less powerful than Germany and Japan, Italy's armed forces played a prominent role during the North African campaign, most notably in the well-fought battle of El Alamein. Despite being initially unprepared for war and facing numerous setbacks, Italy persevered and held its position on multiple fronts throughout the conflict.

Japan's imperial army became infamous for its ruthless tactics as it rampaged through Asia in pursuit of territorial conquests. The well-trained and disciplined soldiers struck fear into their enemies' hearts with their relentless use of unconventional tactics like banzai charges. Their skillful adoption of naval warfare through aircraft carriers proved highly effective in dealing stinging blows to the US Navy at Pearl Harbor.

Notable Militaries: Finland, China, and France

Finland stood as a small but fierce adversary against the Soviet Union during the Winter War of 1939-1940. Despite being vastly outnumbered, they utilized their intimate knowledge of their harsh terrain by employing guerrilla-style tactics like "Motti" that surprised and confounded Soviet forces.

China's presence in World War II is often overshadowed by the major players; however, it was an active participant primarily fighting against Japan. Despite several drawbacks such as a lack of advanced weaponry and poor organization, Chinese forces held out for eight grueling years proving themselves resourceful against heavy odds.

France is often criticized for its quick capitulation after being invaded by Nazi Germany; nevertheless, it is crucial to remember that the French Resistance played a critical role in undermining German authority from within occupied France. While not a traditional military force, they were fiercely committed to the war effort and contributed significantly to the Allied victory.

Technological Advancements, Warfare Strategies, and Global Impact

One notable technological advancement during World War II period was the development of radar technology. Radar - an acronym for radio detection and ranging - allowed for the detection and tracking of enemy aircraft, ships, and other objects using radio waves. This breakthrough powered pivotal victories as it increased situational awareness on the battlefield. Both the Allies and Axis powers made use of radar systems throughout the war, which proved crucial in many campaigns.

Additionally, cryptography played a significant role in World War II. The Allies' decryption of encrypted communication from Axis forces facilitated their understanding of enemy movements and plans. Most famously, British codebreakers at Bletchley Park cracked Germany's Enigma code machine - a feat that greatly impacted the course of the conflict.

World War II also saw great strides in aviation technology. The development of long-range bombers enabled strategic bombing campaigns, which crippled enemy infrastructure and weakened their capabilities for retaliation. The British Avro Lancaster and American Boeing B-29 Superfortress were among these heavy bombers that proved pivotal to the Allied victory. Moreover, jet propulsion began its debut during this time with German-made Messerschmitt Me 262 jet fighters taking to the skies. These advancements set the stage for modern aerial combat.

Warfare strategies likewise evolved significantly during World War II. Blitzkrieg, or "lightning war," marks a key strategy implemented by Germany during their invasion of Western Europe. It focused on rapid mobility, coordinated air support, and concentrated firepower to overwhelm enemy forces quickly and decisively. The tactic proved effective in early campaigns such as the invasion of Poland in 1939 and the fall of France in 1940.

Additionally, island hopping emerged as a prominent strategy employed by the United States in the Pacific campaign. Rather than contesting every Japanese-held island, the U.S. military opted to leapfrog strategically insignificant islands and focus efforts on key targets. By eliminating heavy resistance and reducing overall casualties, this approach enabled the Allies to gain crucial territory without being bogged down in protracted guerilla warfare.

Amphibious assaults also played a crucial role in World War II; one such example was Operation Overlord, more commonly known as D-Day. On June 6, 1944, over 150,000 Allied troops descended upon the beaches of Normandy, France. This large-scale amphibious assault marked a turning point in the war, as it led to significant gains on Western Front and ultimately contributed to the eventual defeat of Nazi Germany.

Lastly, World War II brought forth arguably one of the most consequential technologies in human history: atomic weapons. In August 1945, toward the end of the conflict, the United States dropped two powerful atomic bombs on Hiroshima and Nagasaki. These bombings wreaked devastating destruction on Japanese cities and led to Japan's unconditional surrender days later. The nuclear age had dawned.

The cataclysmic effects of World War II spread far beyond its theaters of battle. The war effectively restructured international politics into a bipolar world order, shaped primarily by two superpowers - the United States and Soviet Union. Moreover, amidst widespread devastation and casualties exceeding 70 million lives lost worldwide, nations emerged determined to build lasting institutions that would prevent further global conflicts. This desire resulted in organizations such as the United Nations and NATO.

Exploration of the Holocaust and War Crimes

The Holocaust is undeniably one of the most harrowing and catastrophic events in human history. As World War II raged on between the Axis and Allied Powers, a sinister genocide unfolded behind the scenes, orchestrated by Adolf Hitler's Nazi regime. In 1933, as Hitler rose to power and established his dictatorial government, he began to systematically persecute Jews under the guise of creating a utopian society. Anti-Semitic legislation was enacted, leading to widespread discrimination against Jewish citizens. Initially, these actions were solely restricted to laws that barred Jews from certain occupations or owning specific types of property; but soon enough, they escalated into something far worse.

The Holocaust took shape as Hitler initiated his "Final Solution," which aimed at eliminating all Jews within territories under Nazi control. Estimated figures show that approximately six million Jews perished in the genocide – a number that accounts for two-thirds of European Jewry at the time.

Throughout World War II, concentration camps were constructed across Europe. These camps varied in function and cruelty – some served as forced labor centers for Jewish prisoners, while others were explicitly designed for mass extermination through gas chambers or shooting squads. Notorious examples include Auschwitz-Birkenau, Treblinka, and Sobibor.

The horrors of these camps are difficult to fathom; men, women, and children were forcibly piled into ghettos before being systematically eradicated. The SS (Schutzstaffel) soldiers ruthlessly transported victims to death camps via cattle cars in the now-notorious process known as "deportation."

Amidst this unfathomable darkness, acts of bravery shone bright as individuals risked their lives to save fellow human beings from certain death. People like Oskar Schindler, Raoul Wallenberg, and Sir Nicholas Winton have been recognized for their tireless efforts to protect and save Jewish lives.

Unfortunately, the Holocaust wasn't the only atrocity committed during World War II. The conflict witnessed numerous war crimes from all sides.

In the Pacific Theater, Japanese forces engaged in several notorious war crimes. These include the Rape of Nanking, where Japanese soldiers raped and murdered between 40,000 to 300,000 Chinese civilians in a six-week period; forced labor of POWs (prisoners of war) along the Burma Railway; and horrific medical experiments conducted by Unit 731 on thousands of victims.

On the Eastern Front, Soviet forces perpetrated crimes against humanity as well. Reports document mass rapes of German women as they advanced into German territory, summary executions of prisoners, as well as intentional destruction of civilian areas as part of the scorched earth policy.

Meanwhile, Allied forces were not free from their own violations. The firebombing campaigns that targeted cities such as Hamburg, Tokyo, Dresden, and Hiroshima resulted in extensive civilian deaths. Strategic bombing missions often disregarded their impact on civilian populations and infrastructure – policies that have raised moral questions surrounding these actions ever since.

Accountability came in the wake of World War II with war crime trials held to prosecute those responsible for these horrific acts. In Nuremberg and Tokyo Trial proceedings, major political and military leaders were indicted. This was a vital step in global reparations, acknowledging these horrific episodes within our shared past – a testament to attaining international justice.

Cold War Militaries

Review Of Superpower Militaries: United States Vs. Soviet Union

The Cold War period, from the late 1940s to the early 1990s, witnessed an intense rivalry between two global superpowers, the United States and the Soviet Union. This era saw an unparalleled build-up of military strength by both nations, focusing on nuclear weaponry, espionage, and global influence.

Both superpowers perceived each other as existential threats and recognized that the balance of power had shifted by World War II's end. The strategic imperative to project strength while avoiding direct conflict was driven by ideological differences and divergent global ambitions. This tension manifested in various proxy wars, arms races, and technological advancements that would redefine warfare for decades.

The United States military during the Cold War underwent a significant transformation to adapt to the emerging challenges posed by a bipolar world order. The establishment of the North Atlantic Treaty Organization (NATO) in 1949 provided a collective defense system that enabled US forces to expand their reach into Europe. New branches, such as the US Air Force, emerged in response to rapid technological developments. Among its greatest achievements was superiority in strategic bomber technology with aircraft such as the B-52 Stratofortress providing long-range nuclear strike capabilities.

Additionally, the United States developed a robust naval force that could exert influence worldwide through aircraft carrier battle groups. It commissioned advanced warships like the Nimitz-class carriers and Arleigh Burke-class destroyers to maintain power projection capabilities, ensuring dominance over open oceans and key maritime chokepoints.

The US Army played a crucial role in implementing containment strategy against potential Soviet aggression aimed at halting communism's spread across Europe. Countering this threat necessitated a large standing army available for rapid deployment during times of crisis.

On the other side of the spectrum, the Soviet Union consolidated its military might under the Red Army's banner. Soviet planners implemented a series of five-year plans to modernize their military in line with technological advances made during World War II. This resulted in one of the largest militaries in history, with a combination of conventional and nuclear forces that posed an ongoing challenge to American strategic planners.

The Soviet Union's disciplined ground forces prioritized mass infantry supported by potent armor divisions such as the T-34 and T-72 tanks, complemented by a mobilized reserve well-versed in home-field defense. The Red Army laid particular emphasis on artillery, often employing it on a massive scale, distinguishing itself from the US Army's more flexible and maneuver-oriented focus.

The Soviet Air Force counterparts focused primarily on interceptors designed to defend against potential airborne threats such as U-2 spy planes or B-52 bombers. Notable examples include the MiG-21 Fishbed and Su-27 Flanker fighter aircraft.

The USSR also constructed a formidable navy but remained limited by geographical constraints that impeded power projection beyond local coastal waters. Consequently, their fleets tended to be defensively oriented, emphasizing strike capabilities with platforms like submarines armed with nuclear missiles (SSBNs) and anti-shipping cruise missiles (ASCMs). One notable Cold War deterrent was its enormous Typhoon-class nuclear-powered ballistic missile submarine.

Crucial to both militaries' strategies was the development and deployment of nuclear weapons. The United States maintained a triad of air, sea, and land-based delivery systems such as intercontinental ballistic missiles (ICBMs), submarine-launched ballistic missiles (SLBMs), and strategic bombers to ensure second-strike capability and deterrence against Soviet aggression. In response, the USSR developed ICBMs like the R-7 Semyorka and fostered an extensive network of early warning radar stations designed to detect potential enemy attacks.

Overall, the United States and Soviet Union's Cold War militaries represented a strategic standoff between two titanic superpowers, each constantly adjusting their strategic posture in the face of rapidly shifting global dynamics. These forces remain influential in contemporary armed forces' strategies and continue to shape our understanding of military power and conflict in the 20th century's latter half.

Key Proxy Conflicts and Related Military Forces

The Cold War era witnessed several proxy conflicts as both superpowers sought to expand their sphere of influence without engaging in direct military confrontation. This section discusses the key proxy conflicts in the context of the Cold War, namely the Korean War and Vietnam War, and related military forces that shaped the world during this period.

The Korean War (1950-1953), often referred to as "The Forgotten War," was a significant conflict that emerged in the early years of the Cold War. This war was triggered when North Korean forces, backed by Soviet Union and China, invaded South Korea, seeking unification under a communist government. In response, an international coalition led by the United States intervened on behalf of South Korea under United Nations' auspices.

Military forces from various countries participated in this bloody conflict. The South Korean military (The Republic of Korea Armed

Forces) demonstrated its tenacity and gradually improved its operational capabilities with the support from the US-led coalition. Meanwhile, North Korean forces (the Korean People's Army) were well-trained, numerous, and equipped with advanced Soviet-supplied weaponry.

These opposing forces were supported by major international players. The US-led coalition included American troops as part of the United Nations Command (UNC), which spearheaded military operations against North Korean forces. The People's Volunteer Army (PVA), a Chinese force disguised as non-state combatants, provided substantial support to North Korea.

The conflict resulted in a protracted stalemate around the 38th parallel – which divided North and South Korea before the war – effectively leading to an uneasy ceasefire through the 1953 armistice agreement. The devastating human toll and catastrophic impact on both nations' infrastructures are still felt today with Korea remaining divided.

Another significant proxy conflict during the Cold War was the Vietnam War (1955-1975) between communist forces of North Vietnam and South Vietnam's authoritarian government backed by the United States. This prolonged conflict symbolizes the complexities that characterized Cold War military interventions, marked by ideological struggle, global power play, and pervasive influence on domestic affairs of countries involved.

The primary military players during the Vietnam War included North Vietnam's military, known as the People's Army of Vietnam (PAVN), and their allies - the Viet Cong. This well-organized force employed guerilla tactics against both enemy combatants and civilians who supported the opposing side, aided by supply routes like the infamous Ho Chi Minh trail traversing from North to South.

South Vietnamese forces, known as Army of the Republic of Vietnam (ARVN), were backed by US military intervention through air support, special operations groups like "MACV-SOG," and ground troops. Although South Vietnamese forces showcased incremental improvements in their combat capacity, political instability at home constrained their overall strategic effectiveness.

Other foreign nations also participated in this conflict to support either side. The Soviet Union and its allies backed North Vietnam through military advisors and weaponry, while Australia, New Zealand, South Korea, Thailand, and other countries sent ground troops or other assistance to bolster South Vietnamese efforts.

The final moments of this conflict culminated when North Vietnamese forces launched a massive offensive in 1975, eventually capturing Saigon, which led to unification under communist rule. The war's ramifications extended beyond Southeast Asia with widespread protests and global dissatisfaction with US war policies.

The Nuclear Arms Race and Mutually Assured Destruction

The nuclear arms race was a fundamental aspect of the Cold War, a period of ideological and geopolitical confrontation between the United States and the Soviet Union that lasted from the end of World War II until the late 1980s. It was marked by the competing development and stockpiling of nuclear weapons, with both superpowers attempting to dominate each other's military capabilities while avoiding direct conflict to prevent complete obliteration.

In this tumultuous era, national security relied on a delicate balance of power, exemplified by the concept of mutually assured destruction (MAD). This doctrine posited that any attack using nuclear weapons would result in a response sufficient to cause total destruction for both aggressor and defender alike. The devastation would be so absolute that it was assumed no rational actor would engage in nuclear warfare, creating a tense yet stable condition.

Several essential developments contributed to the inception and evolution of the nuclear arms race. In August 1945, at the tail end of World War II, the United States dropped atomic bombs on Hiroshima and Nagasaki, instantaneously demonstrating their unprecedented destructive potential. This prompted an urgent push for nuclear development in other countries, particularly in the Soviet Union, which successfully detonated its first atomic bomb in 1949.

Fueled by parallel fears and ambitions, both nations engaged in an accelerating competition to build a more potent arsenal. Early stages of this race saw significant advancements such as hydrogen bombs – far more powerful than their atomic counterparts – successfully tested by both countries in 1952 (US) and 1953 (USSR).

Throughout the following decades, technological breakthroughs perpetuated a relentless pursuit for tactical supremacy. Missiles became increasingly sophisticated with intercontinental ballistic missiles (ICBMs), submarine-launched ballistic missiles (SLBMs), and multiple independently targetable reentry vehicles (MIRVs), which enabled multiple warheads to be carried on a single missile. Missile defense systems were also established to guard against incoming strikes.

This constant expansion of destructive power reached a critical point during the Cuban Missile Crisis in 1962 when the world stood at the brink of nuclear catastrophe. The discovery of Soviet nuclear missiles in Cuba, a mere ninety miles from American shores, triggered alarm amongst US authorities, who resolved to confront the threat head-on. A tense thirteen-day standoff ensued, during which neither side relented until the Soviets ultimately agreed to remove their offensive weaponry from Cuba in return for American withdrawal of intermediate-range ballistic missiles from Turkey and Italy.

The anxiety pervading this confrontation, initiated discussions about strategic arms control as both nations recognized that measures must be taken to mitigate the risk of inadvertent nuclear destruction.

Consequently, a series of agreements were negotiated, starting with the Partial Nuclear Test Ban Treaty in 1963 and followed by further treaties like Strategic Arms Limitation Talks (SALT) I in 1972 and SALT II in 1979.

These attempts at diplomacy marked an acknowledgement that an unbridled arms race could jeopardize global security. Nevertheless, advances persisted as new strategies emerged such as the Anti-Ballistic Missile (ABM) Treaty of 1972, forcing both superpowers to adapt their approaches while maintaining equilibrium.

Ultimately, it was this unwavering pursuit of balance that precluded nuclear annihilation during the Cold War; any deviation threatened catastrophe. The concept of mutually assured destruction served as an uneasy deterrent that maintained peace amid powerful tensions between the United States and Soviet Union. Their acknowledgment that victory was unattainable without complete destruction thrust both nations into a precarious stalemate, where they remained until diplomatic efforts replaced military aggression as progress emerged toward disarmament and détente.

Modern Era and Contemporary Militaries

Discussion Of Current Military Powers

The interconnected nature of the modern era has given rise to some remarkable military powers, each wielding unprecedented capabilities to protect their nations and project influence. The United States is by far the world's most significant military superpower. Its armed forces are organized under the Department of Defense, comprising the Army, Navy, Air Force, Marine Corps, and Coast Guard. Currently, the United States boasts a defense budget of approximately $740 billion, enabling them to possess state-of-the-art weaponry and cutting-edge technology. The US military also maintains a vast network of bases worldwide, allowing them to project power efficiently. It is this unparalleled strength that makes the United States' military presence one of immense strategic importance.

China has emerged as a prominent global power rivaling that of the United States. Its rapid economic development over recent decades have allowed it to invest heavily in its military capabilities. The People's Liberation Army (PLA) is now one of the largest and most technologically advanced armed forces globally. The Chinese military consists of various services: the PLA Ground Force (PLAGF), PLA Navy (PLAN), PLA Air Force (PLAAF), and PLA Rocket Force (PLARF). Recently, China has increased spending in areas such as its navy and air force capabilities, aiming at asserting control over its sphere of influence exerted through its ambitious Belt and Road Initiative.

Russia is another noteworthy military power with an extensive history of martial prowess inherited from its status as a former world superpower. Despite hiccups in military development following the

Soviet Union's dissolution, Russia has managed to maintain a robust global presence through significant investment in its armed forces. The Russian Federation's Armed Forces consist of three branches: Ground Forces, Aerospace Forces (combining Air Force and Aerospace Defense Forces), and the Navy. Additionally, Russia boasts a sizeable nuclear arsenal that ensures it remains a key player in global geopolitics. Its military focus has recently shifted towards developing long-range precision strike capabilities and enhancing electronic warfare systems.

NATO, formally known as the North Atlantic Treaty Organization, is a political and military alliance comprising 30 member countries. Established in 1949, NATO strives to provide a collective defense mechanism against any threat a member might face. With the United States being its spearhead ally, NATO possesses sophisticated and technologically advanced military assets to ensure the alliance's potency in modern warfare. Member nations contribute their armed forces personnel on rotational deployments, enabling rapid response and cooperation among allies.

These four contemporary military forces possess distinct strengths and capabilities in various combinations that make them formidable on the global stage. The United States' unparalleled dominance results from its ability to leverage technological advancements and effectively coordinate its various military branches. Consequently, the US remains at the forefront of global defense innovations.

China's rapid rise as a global power has come with extensive reforms within its military industrial complex; however, some shortcomings persist compared to its US counterpart — especially when examining their global network of bases which currently pales in comparison.

Russia, despite facing setbacks in economic development and defense industry challenges, has managed to retain significant influence on the world stage through sheer determination and military innovation — particularly in modern weaponry like hypersonic missiles.

NATO's collective defense also demonstrates strategic advantages by relying on cooperation among member countries — an essential ingredient for enhanced response capabilities and shared situational awareness.

Emphasis On Modern Warfare, Cyber Capabilities, And Geopolitical Influence

The trajectory of military power has shifted from conventional forces to modern warfare systems, characterized by an increased reliance on cyber capabilities and cutting-edge technology. Over the centuries, militaries have evolved dramatically with advances in weaponry and battle strategies. However, as this transformation continues, so does the importance of geopolitical influence in shaping the outcomes of conflicts and global power dynamics.

Modern warfare encompasses a wide range of techniques that involve the use of advanced technology and innovative tactics to gain an advantage over adversaries. One key component is the role of unmanned systems or drones in reconnaissance operations, precision strikes and even swarming attacks that can overwhelm enemy defenses. The steady growth in autonomous capabilities allows militaries to minimize casualties while enhancing surveillance and response capacities.

Furthermore, information dominance has become crucial in modern warfare. Command and control systems are now designed not only for real-time communication but also for processing vast amounts of data gathered from various sources such as satellites, sensors, and intelligence reports. The increasing prevalence of network-centric warfare precludes the need for agile decision-making based on accurate situational awareness.

In tandem with these technological advancements comes a greater emphasis on special operations forces (SOF). SOF units employ unconventional methods that prioritize stealth, speed, and surgical precision over brute strength. Their highly trained operatives can effectively infiltrate enemy territory undetected or disrupt hostile activities without resorting to large-scale conventional assaults.

Cyber capabilities have emerged as a critical factor in determining a nation's military prowess. In today's interconnected world, the power to infiltrate an adversary's digital networks and extract valuable information—or launch destructive attacks—has become indispensable. Cyber warfare can deliver crippling effects without relying on conventional armed forces.

State-sponsored cyber-espionage facilitates the theft of classified data, granting valuable insights into an opponent's weaknesses and planning. By interdicting digital systems, cyber-attacks could disable air defense networks, disrupt communications, and compromise infrastructure; creating chaos on the home front that cripples the enemy's ability to respond in physical battlespaces.

Geopolitical influence complements the advances in modern warfare and cyber capabilities by allowing countries to project power globally. Through diplomacy, economic prowess, and strategic alliances, influential nations have gained the leverage necessary to assert their interests wherever they see fit. The role of military bases abroad highlights this notion, as they extend a nation's strategic reach into regions that may be far from its own borders.

As we have seen with recent conflicts involving major powers, hybrid tactics have also become more prevalent. This involves employing a mix of conventional forces, irregular fighters, proxy militias and cyber-operations, blurring the lines between states and non-state actors. Coupled with strategic disinformation campaigns aimed at disrupting an enemy's decision-making process, these methods add another layer of complexity to modern warfare.

This combination of modern warfare systems, cyber capabilities and geopolitical influence is reshaping global military dynamics in ways that are both challenging conventional notions of military might and forging new frontiers for conflict resolution. No longer limited to direct confrontations on the battlefield or measured solely in terms of physical assets, today's military forces defy traditional definitions.

Rather than signaling the end of conventional armies or large-scale invasions, these developments demand a reevaluation and rethinking of how militaries might operate in future conflicts. In this constantly evolving landscape of power struggles and high-stakes competitive interactions between nations, all parties must contend with unprecedented levels of sophistication and complexity.

Modern Era and Contemporary Military Challenges

Throughout history, the military landscape has experienced multiple changes. The cost of these adaptations is often high, as combatants constantly vie for supremacy while exploiting each other's weaknesses. In the modern era, new military challenges have arisen in the form of terrorism, piracy, and hybrid warfare. These contemporary threats test the prowess and resilience of even the most advanced forces of our time.

Terrorism has represented a consistent challenge to stability and security over the past century. Technological advancements have exacerbated its impact by providing non-state actors with access to powerful weapons and capabilities once reserved for nation-states; guns, bombs, and communication technologies enable low-cost offensive operations that can inflict significant damage on both the enemy's infrastructure and psyche.

As global society evolves to counteract these threats, terrorists continue to adapt their tactics, often turning to suicide attacks or hostage-taking situations as a means to create fear and panic. These asymmetric tactics make it difficult for traditional militaries to conduct decisive military operations without causing collateral damage or harming innocent civilians. Furthermore, terrorism capitalizes on complex political factors including ethnic tensions and geopolitical strife, contributing to persistent intimidation and potentially opening avenues for more malicious advances.

Piracy represents another serious threat in the contemporary world. Historically viewed as a lesser menace operating primarily at sea, today's pirates have evolved into sophisticated networks engaged in organized crime. They threaten maritime trade routes—the lifeblood of international commerce—and exploit weak governance structures in certain regions.

Modern-day piracy now extends beyond ransom attempts at hijacking ships to include attacks on undersea communication cables and oil pipelines. To combat this menace, naval forces use advanced technologies such as unmanned aerial vehicles (UAVs) and satellite reconnaissance systems while working closely with civilian agencies to enhance coordinated responses. However, piracy remains a challenging issue fueled by economic inequality, insufficient law enforcement resources in struggling territories, and a demand for black market goods.

Hybrid warfare is yet another challenge faced by contemporary military forces. This form of conflict fuses both conventional and unconventional warfare elements, employing tactics ranging from cyber and electronic warfare to psychological operations aimed at sowing discord within enemy territory. Hybrid warfare is an opportunistic approach that allows a less powerful adversary to circumvent the traditional strengths of larger opponents.

An example of hybrid warfare can be seen in Russia's annexation of Crimea. The Russian military used a blend of diplomacy, propaganda, and special forces intervention to achieve their objectives while avoiding open confrontation with NATO. Loads of misinformation circulated throughout the region, making it difficult for an international response to develop a coherent strategy, ultimately rendering them ineffective.

Addressing hybrid warfare demands flexibility and adaptability from military structures and strategies. Combatants must evolve their thought patterns to consider these multi-domain threats and develop effective countermeasures.

As militaries confront the challenges posed by terrorism, piracy, and hybrid warfare in the contemporary world, they are forced to reinvent their models of operation – exploring methods that are less dependent on brute force and more situated in intelligence gathering, lateral thinking, and cooperation between nation-states. These collaborative trends signal an era of shared responsibility where great militaries navigate complex operational environments that defy the boundaries of traditional combat.

Although historical battles have demanded tremendous skill from notable warriors and commanders, contemporary military encounters require a new breed of strategic genius: the ability to adapt intelligently to an ever-changing landscape while leveraging advanced technologies against highly adaptive adversaries.

Modern militaries need leaders who can think creatively as they navigate through complex ethical dilemmas while balancing economic resources against national security interests. As global power dynamics continue to evolve and new forms of conflict emerge in the modern era, we honor the rich history of those forces who have faced adversity with unmatched resolve – setting the stage for today's greatest military minds to prevail over contemporary challenges.

Beyond Borders: Unconventional Militaries and Insurgent Forces

Exploration of Non-State Actors, Insurgent Groups, and Unconventional Warfare Tactics

Warfare has primarily been associated with state actors engaging in battle on conventional grounds, utilizing hierarchical command structures and traditional maneuvers. However, as the nature of conflict evolved, so did the tactics and strategies employed by non-state actors and insurgent groups.

Non-state actors are entities that sit outside the jurisdiction of national governments. They consist of political organizations, rebel groups, terrorist cells, militias, and transnational criminal organizations. These groups often employ unconventional warfare tactics to achieve their objectives and ensure their survivability against more powerful opponents.

Unconventional warfare is a form of conflict where non-traditional combat tactics and strategies are utilized by a smaller force to gain advantage over a larger or technologically superior opponent. The purpose of unconventional warfare is to exploit weaknesses in an enemy's defenses, capabilities, or morale through asymmetric means.

One of the most renowned non-state actors in history was the Scottish rebel, William Wallace. Faced with a vastly superior English force during the First War of Scottish Independence (1296–1328), Wallace led his troops by employing guerrilla tactics to great effect. Utilizing ambushes, hit-and-run raids, and misdirection, Wallace successfully fought for Scotland's freedom against all odds.

Similarly, during the Vietnam War (1955–1975), Viet Cong guerrillas engaged in unconventional warfare to resist American forces. Employing booby traps, ambushes, tunnel networks, and espionage activities to support North Vietnamese forces on conventional battlefields. Leveraging on their intimate knowledge of local geography and inventive strategies allowed these small units to disrupt seemingly unstoppable American forces for years.

Insurgent groups often require access to resources that support their growth and development. For this reason, they rely on various funding mechanisms such as black-market trading, taxation of local populations, and smuggling operations. Throughout history, non-state actors have been able to leverage these methods to fuel their campaigns.

Take the Italian mafia for example; it has deep-rooted connections within the country's political, economic, and social structures that enable it to operate beyond the reach of Italian law enforcement. By generating income through illicit means, mafia organizations could fund their brand of unconventional warfare.

The Revolutionary Armed Forces of Colombia (FARC) is another case in point. Its existence was sustained for decades through drug trafficking, extortion, and seizing territory from the Colombian government. Using these resources, the FARC waged a brutal guerrilla campaign against both Colombian authorities and rival groups throughout its history.

Unconventional warfare tactics have evolved over time as well. Modern-day insurgent groups are known to incorporate information warfare into their strategies by utilizing social media platforms and other digital avenues to propagate their message. The digital age has allowed insurgents to recruit new members globally, disseminate misinformation to disrupt enemy operations, and even conduct cyber-espionage activities.

Perhaps one of the most prominent examples of an insurgent group utilizing digital means is the Islamic State (ISIS). They employed various online platforms to recruit supporters and spread propaganda materials in multiple languages. This digital media strategy allowed them to access vast new audiences worldwide, bolstering their ranks with fighters from many different nations.

Case Studies on Guerrilla Warfare, Terrorism, And Cyber Threats

In modern times, no comprehensive exploration of military history would be complete without delving into the complexities of guerrilla warfare, terrorism, and cyber threats. This SECTION scrutinizes three significant case studies that have altered the landscape of warfare in undeniable ways: the Viet Cong's guerrilla campaign during the Vietnam War; Al Qaeda's breakthrough terrorist attack on September 11, 2001; and Russia's alleged interference in the 2016 U.S. Presidential Election.

Guerrilla Warfare: The Vietnam War

The Vietnam War (1955–1975) was a critical example of asymmetric warfare that pitted the US-led coalition against the communist forces of North Vietnam and Viet Cong guerrillas in the South. Despite having superior military technology and resources at their disposal, US forces struggled to suppress the guerrilla tactics employed by their adversaries.

Often operating out of underground tunnel networks and blending in with civilian populations, Viet Cong fighters utilized hit-and-run attacks and ambushes to disrupt American supply lines, wear down enemy morale, and force decisionmakers into a war of attrition. The dense jungles and harsh terrain of Vietnam only compounded these difficulties for American troops. Ultimately, this unconventional approach played a significant role in undermining US efforts to achieve victory in Vietnam.

Terrorism: The September 11 Attacks

On September 11, 2001, a series of coordinated terrorist attacks by the Islamist extremist group al-Qaeda shook the United States. Hijackers commandeered four commercial airliners, crashing two planes into the Twin Towers in New York City and another into the Pentagon; a fourth flight was brought down by passengers thwarting an attack on a target in Washington D.C., ultimately crashing in Pennsylvania.

The attacks led to the deaths of nearly 3,000 people and caused a significant shift in global security policies. They demonstrated that non-state actors could orchestrate asymmetric attacks on superpowers like the United States, undermining conventional military paradigms.

In response to these events, President George W. Bush launched the "War on Terror," mobilizing military forces with global partnerships to combat Islamist terrorism. The 9/11 attacks reshaped American foreign policy, defense strategies, and civil liberties during the 21st century as concerns over security took precedence.

Cyber Threats: The Stuxnet Worm

The Stuxnet worm, discovered in 2010, deactivated thousands of centrifuges used for uranium enrichment in Iran's Natanz nuclear facility and is considered a hallmark of cyber warfare's potential for disrupting infrastructure systems. Although the exact origins of Stuxnet remain hidden, it is widely believed to have been developed by the United States and Israel as a strategic effort to delay Iran's nuclear program without resorting to traditional airstrikes or land invasion.

Stuxnet demonstrated that cyber attackers can exploit weaknesses in critical industrial systems, causing cascading damage through malware or viruses, disrupting physical infrastructure, and potentially leading to catastrophic consequences. Cyber threats have underscored the importance of robust digital security in addition to traditional military methods for combating adversaries and protecting nation-states in the digital age.

Guerrilla warfare, terrorism, and cyber threats represent some of the most significant challenges militaries have faced over time. The Vietnam War showcased the impact of guerrilla tactics on conventional superpowers, while September 11 highlighted the potential devastation terrorists could inflict using asymmetrical warfare tactics even against an enemy with immense military might. Meanwhile, the Stuxnet worm laid bare the vulnerabilities nation-states faced from cyberattacks.

These examples emphasize the need for modern military forces to adapt beyond conventional means to confront emerging threats effectively. As contemporary conflicts blur martial boundaries, global security depends on understanding these myriad challenges and devising strategies capable of addressing them.

Examination of Paramilitary Forces and Their Influence on Armed Conflicts

Paramilitary forces have roots dating back as far as ancient times, with irregular auxiliary units often supporting professional armies. Such forces emerged in various eras and civilizations, including Ancient Rome, China's Warring States period, and Medieval Europe. The term "paramilitary" itself is derived from the Greek word "paramilitos," which translates to "near the military." This definition reflects the nature of these units functioning somewhere between civilian and military organizations.

The rise of nationalism and political movements in the 20th century heightened the importance of paramilitary groups. They infiltrated almost every continent, with prominent examples being Germany's Freikorps – which later evolved into the Nazi stormtroopers – Italy's Fascist Blackshirts, and Latin America's numerous anti-communist death squads. Often operating in unstable or politically charged environments, these forces played decisive roles in maintaining or toppling governments.

One crucial factor that separates paramilitary units from regular armed forces is their level of independence. Often receiving funding, weapons, or intelligence from state actors or well-established organizations, these groups are relatively free from governmental oversight or direct control. This autonomy allows them to operate beyond borders and carry out covert missions that may be too politically sensitive for state military action.

Paramilitary units also distinguish themselves by employing unconventional tactics that capitalize on their agility and adaptability– characteristics often lacking in traditional military structures. These groups have proven adept at utilizing guerrilla warfare, sabotage, infiltration, and psychological operations to demoralize and disrupt enemy forces.

The impact of paramilitary forces on armed conflicts throughout history is vast and varied. Some groups have participated in liberation struggles for their countries, such as the Viet Cong in Vietnam or the Irish Republican Army during the Irish War of Independence. Others have served as state-sponsored agents, enacting policies of repression, intimidation, and violence upon opposition groups – the Selous Scouts in Rhodesia, for example, who were used to suppress rebel factions fighting against the settler-led government.

However, not all paramilitary forces serve purely nationalist or political agendas. Many such groups have entered conflicts due to a sense of loyalty to their community or a desire for personal gain. Private military contractors (PMCs), like Blackwater Worldwide or Executive Outcomes, have thrived in conflict-ridden regions as they offer security services for profit. In these cases, allegiance is dictated by financial incentives rather than ideological devotion.

As global conflict becomes more complex and intertwined with politics and geopolitical interests, the influence of paramilitary forces will continue to grow. Some argue that governments should capitalize on their expertise and skills by incorporating them into formal military structures; others believe they should be reined in and sanctioned as destabilizing elements.

Regardless of where one stands on this issue, the fact remains that these unconventional warriors hold significant power. Their operations beyond borders exemplify both the fluidity and unpredictability of modern warfare. The *"100 Greatest Militaries Throughout History"* would be a vastly different list without the inclusion and recognition of paramilitary forces that have shifted the tides of conflict across continents and eras.

Military Innovations and Future Trends

Cutting-Edge Military Technologies and Innovations

As we study the 100 greatest of militaries throughout history, it becomes increasingly apparent that technology and innovation have been vital drivers of military supremacy. Here, we will examine some of the most groundbreaking and cutting-edge military technologies, which have the potential to revolutionize warfare soon.

Drones: Revolutionizing Aerial Warfare

Unmanned aerial vehicles (UAVs), commonly known as drones, have drastically changed the face of aerial warfare. With their ability to fly for extended periods without putting pilots at risk, drones offer significant advantages in terms of surveillance, reconnaissance, and targeted strikes. Nations with sophisticated drone technology can monitor enemy activities and gather valuable intelligence, while also delivering precision strikes with minimal collateral damage.

Drones are classified into various categories based on their size, payload capacity, range, and endurance. As technology advances, military drones are becoming more versatile and lethal. For example, some drones can perform coordinated swarm attacks or can communicate with other drones and human controllers in real-time. This provides ground troops with crucial situational awareness and reduces response times during combat operations.

Space Warfare: The Next Frontier

The vast expanse of space holds untold potential for military dominance. As human capabilities expand beyond Earth and into the cosmos, an entirely new arena for warfare emerges – space warfare.

The militarization of space has become a critical component of national security strategies worldwide.

Satellite systems play an indispensable part in modern combat operations as they enable global positioning, navigation, weather monitoring, communication links, and reconnaissance capabilities. These invaluable assets are alluring targets for adversaries looking to disrupt or eliminate these strategic advantages.

Moreover, with nations developing space-based weapons that could potentially target terrestrial assets or other satellites makes it imperative to maintain situational awareness in orbit. Anti-satellite weapons (ASAT), such as missiles or directed energy weapons, could be used to degrade, or destroy enemy reconnaissance, communication, and navigation satellites. Defense against such threats would involve developing countermeasures to protect space-based assets or deploying alternative platforms that can quickly replace the lost capabilities.

Hypersonic Weapons: A New Generation of Speed and Lethality

Hypersonic weapons are a class of long-range, high-speed missiles designed to deliver explosive payloads at speeds exceeding Mach 5. These weapons can evade conventional missile defense systems due to their exceptional speed and unpredictable flight trajectory. The velocity at which they travel means that hypersonic weapons reach distant targets much faster than traditional ballistic missiles and give adversaries much less time to react.

Creating operational hypersonic weapons is a top priority for militaries around the world, with significant investments being made in research and development. One area where hypersonic vehicles excel is in strike capabilities. Hypersonic cruise missiles and glide vehicles can pierce advanced air defenses with ease, due to their ability to change altitude and course mid-flight.

Advanced Armor and Exoskeletons

The protection of soldiers has always been paramount in military operations, leading to technological advancements in personal armor and equipment. Future infantry units may be equipped with advanced exoskeletons - wearable carbon nanotube suits designed to enhance soldiers' physical capabilities, such as strength, endurance, and agility. These suits can also incorporate sensors for monitoring the wearer's health status and provide essential biometric data to medical personnel in real-time.

Additionally, advancements in material science have allowed researchers to develop next-generation armor composites that offer improved protection against small arms fire and explosives. This could lead to the deployment of lighter, more durable body armor capable of minimizing harm from various threats encountered in the battlefield.

These cutting-edge military innovations have the potential to shape the future of warfare by providing nations with the capabilities necessary for strategic dominance over adversaries during conflict. As research continues and technology advances further, it remains to be seen how the landscape of military power will evolve, but one thing is certain - technology and innovation will remain key factors in deciding the fate of battles and wars.

Speculation on Future Trends and Potential Shifts in Global Military Dominance

As history has shown, trends in military warfare are ever-changing, driven by advances in technology, ideological shifts, and geopolitical rivalry. The first major trend is the increased reliance on unmanned systems and robotics as part of modern warfare. Countries with advanced military capabilities are embracing drone technology for surveillance purposes, reconnaissance, strike missions, and even frontline combat. The use of these remotely controlled systems can significantly reduce human risk, while providing highly accurate targeting and intelligence gathering capabilities. However, this growing dependency on technology also raises ethical concerns and may redefine the traditional notion of military engagement.

Another trend likely to shape future military power dynamics is that of artificial intelligence (AI) integration into warfighting strategies. AI-based systems can analyze vast amounts of data at unprecedented speeds, thereby enhancing threat identification and prediction. By integrating AI-based technologies into command-and-control networks, defense personnel can optimize decision-making processes during large-scale operations. This increased efficiency holds the potential to fundamentally alter how combatants wage war.

Moreover, significant advancements in cyber warfare have opened a new frontier for states to wage conflict or defend their interest outside the traditional battlefield. State-sponsored cyber-attacks now target vital infrastructure, such as power grids or telecommunication systems, recognizing their strategic importance. These attacks also breed uncertainty about whether an act constitutes aggression or not. As cyber warfare continues to become increasingly commonplace, states must balance traditional military assets with a robust cyber defense apparatus that addresses ever-evolving threats.

Another crucial factor affecting global military dominance will be heightened competition for resources among major powers as they seek energy security. Throughout history, territorial control has dictated where certain resources lie; however, disputes over maritime boundaries have grown more prevalent in recent times, often due to hydrocarbon exploration or fishing rights. Conflicting claims and the pursuit of critical resources in contested areas may exacerbate existing tensions between nations, potentially leading to the rise of military confrontations surrounding resource allocation and regional hegemony.

In addition, a shifting balance of power among nations will undoubtedly impact global military dominance. The emergence of previously dormant or lesser powers as key actors on the world stage will challenge the status quo. The Asian continent holds relevance in this regard, with countries such as China and India possessing significant economic and military potential. Investment in advanced military assets by these emerging powers could spark serious competition with established global players and force them to adapt their strategic postures accordingly.

Finally, advancing non-state actors require the attention of traditional military forces globally. From terrorist organizations to transnational criminal networks, these groups pose significant challenges to state stability and sovereignty. As they continue to grow and adapt, states must adjust their strategies to better address emerging threats posed by non-state actors who are increasingly resorting to non-traditional tactics like hybrid warfare.

Discerning the precise trajectory of future military trends is inherently uncertain; however, some key patterns are likely to shape the future landscape of global military dominance. Unmanned systems, AI-based technologies, cyber warfare capabilities, competition for resources, shifts in global power dynamics, and advancements in non-state actor threats all serve as vital determinants for how militaries around the world will combat against one another in decades to come.

As we look towards an uncertain future filled with shifting allegiances and evolving technology, it becomes increasingly important for nations to adapt their military strategies not only to maintain their grasp on power but also safeguard their place in this ever-changing world. Ultimately, understanding these trends ensures better preparedness for the unforeseen challenges that lie ahead in global military affairs throughout history's next chapter.

Ethical Considerations for Future Warfare Technologies

As we continue to advance into uncharted territories, ethical considerations must be evaluated cautiously to steer the usage of such technologies. The dawn of autonomous weapon systems has paved the way for swift, efficient, and precise conduct of military operations. Drones and unmanned vehicles possess unprecedented capabilities in both surveillance and offensive actions. This shift away from human combatants raises several pressing ethical concerns. Firstly, it challenges conventional norms regarding accountability in armed conflict. If a drone is responsible for an erroneous attack on civilians or non-combatants, who should be held accountable – the operator, commanding officer, or system programmer?

Embedding complex algorithms into autonomous weapons further expands upon this question of accountability. As these systems learn and adapt from their engagements, traditional lines of responsibility blur. An ethical framework must be established to address this evolving landscape.

In addition to the need for clear accountability protocols, there arises a concern around ensuring respect for human dignity and international humanitarian law (IHL). Fully autonomous weapon systems may struggle to discern between civilians and combatants during hostilities significantly increasing the risk of civilian casualties or disproportional harm. To address these concerns, rigorous testing, guidelines, and safety measures must be established before deploying such systems into battlefields.

Another emerging technology with profound implications for future warfare is cyberwarfare – which extends across multiple spheres such as economic infrastructure, trade policies, and disinformation campaigns that disrupt foreign government functions. Cyberattacks can lead to detrimental consequences affecting civilian life without any engagement on traditional physical battlefronts.

Ethical concerns acutely arise from the inherently indiscriminate nature of cyberattacks which often target crucial systems responsible for managing power grids, water supply or healthcare services, with direct and indirect consequences on civilian life. A well-defined ethical framework must be showcased, outlining the acceptable uses of offensive cyber tools, and stressing the adherence to the principles of non-combatant immunity and proportionality.

Also at the forefront of disruptive innovation is the field of biotechnology. Innovations such as "designer" pathogens or genetically modified soldiers can dramatically alter the dynamics of warfare. However, the potential misuse of such advances sparks a myriad of ethical quandaries.

The creation and deployment of biological agents raise questions around discrimination and indiscriminate suffering, contravening IHL principles. The biological modification of human soldiers, on the other hand, introduces unprecedented ethical dilemmas. Altering a soldier's physical or psychological makeup may enhance combat effectiveness but erodes not just their autonomy but also their innate human dignity.

Finally, space-based military technologies present yet another realm of ethical deliberation. The militarization and weaponization of space pose new challenges in terms of global security and adherence to existing arms control agreements. Ethical considerations must address potential arms races in outer space and guideline adherence to prevent destructive debris proliferation in Earth's orbital plane as a direct result.

Developing an ethical framework that caters to future warfare technologies is not only crucial for maintaining human dignity, but also ensures long-lasting peace, security and stability across the globe. This delicate balancing act requires sustained dialogue among world leaders, military officials, scientists, and civilians alike to address emerging technological advancements in warfare responsibly.

In essence, as we venture further into uncharted technological territory examining the 100 greatest militaries throughout history creates a window into our past – informing us on how best to regulate and guide future advancements. Safeguarding humanity's core values while embracing innovation demonstrates our ever-continuing evolution in maintaining an ethically sustainable society amid emerging threats on our collective horizon.

Conclusion

"The 100 Greatest Militaries Throughout History" covers various militaries from the ancient to the modern era, exploring key strategies, technologies, and battles that have shaped history. In the Ancient Era, influential military forces like the Roman Empire, Persian Empire, and Ancient Chinese Armies laid the foundation for warfare strategies and technologies. The Ancient Near East and Far East witnessed the emergence of military powers like Babylonians, Assyrians, Hittites, early Chinese dynasties, and the rise of the Japanese samurai class.

In the Medieval and Renaissance periods, militaries like the Mongol Empire, Ottoman Empire, and European Powers rose to prominence. Advancements in weaponry, tactics, conquests and the importance of religion and chivalry shaped medieval warfare. The Early Modern Period saw military developments in Europe in the 18th century exemplified by Napoleonic Wars and British Empire's growth. The Industrial Revolution significantly impacted warfare during this period.

Additionally, influential militaristic states such as Marathas, Mughals, Safavids, and African Kingdoms emerged in Asia and Africa during this period. They adopted military technologies influenced by European powers. Latin American Revolutionary Wars also played an important role during this time with prominent leaders like Simón Bolívar and José de San Martín leading independence movements. The 19th Century Imperialism & Colonization delves into the role of major imperial powers such as British Empire and French Empire. It discusses colonial wars and resistance movements which impacted global military landscape. During World War I, militaries such as Entente Powers and Central Powers utilized trench warfare tactics and technological advancements causing significant social, economic, and political consequences.

World War II presented a new era in warfare with influential militaries like Allies and Axis Powers introducing new strategies with a global impact. The Holocaust was a somber aspect of this era consisting of heinous war crimes. Cold War Militaries examines the superpowers United States and Soviet Union, key proxy conflicts like Korean War and Vietnam War, followed by the nuclear arms race. Modern Era focuses on current military powers, modern warfare, cyber capabilities and geopolitical influence tackling challenges like terrorism, piracy, and hybrid warfare. The book then explores unconventional militaries and insurgent forces, including guerrilla warfare and paramilitary forces. Lastly, it discusses military innovations and future trends emphasizing AI, drones and space warfare while addressing ethical considerations for future warfare technologies.

This comprehensive guide showcases how fundamental military power has been at shaping human civilization from its infancy to modern times. By understanding these key points, readers can appreciate the complex interplay of politics, economics, and culture that give rise to some of the most extraordinary military achievements in history.

Reflection On the Evolution of Warfare and Its Impact on History and Geopolitics

As societies emerged and established their power, military prowess became an essential aspect of maintaining control, asserting dominance, and ensuring survival in an ever-evolving world. From antiquity to modern times, we have witnessed remarkable advancements in technology, tactics, and weaponry which in turn has altered the way nations engage with one another. Whether it be Alexander the Great's penetration into Asia or Napoleon Bonaparte's ambition to conquer Europe, leaders have all sought greater supremacy and territorial influence by employing superior military capabilities.

Yet, the evolution of warfare is not without its consequences. The devastation wrought upon by wars doesn't simply lie on battlefields but casts a long shadow over global politics, economics, and societies. With great power comes immense responsibility as nations strive to prevent unnecessary conflicts but at the same time, safeguard their sovereignty.

In our contemporary era, we are faced with newer challenges that demand innovative means of addressing conflicts and ensuring global stability. The advent of cybersecurity threats and escalating proxy wars necessitates a reevaluation of conventional strategies. Nevertheless, acknowledging the historical context detailed in this book allows us to appreciate the dynamically evolving nature of warfare and to recognize its impact on global affairs.

Ultimately, *"The 100 Greatest Militaries Throughout History"* provides you with a comprehensive outlook on how warfare has metamorphosed through various junctures in history. As a reflection on mankind's past triumphs and follies alike, this record urges us to learn from our ancestors' experiences while conscientiously striving for a more peaceful future where such conflicts can be minimized or avoided altogether. As our world continues to change, let us carry forth the wisdom and lessons acquired from our past to shape a harmonious and sustainable geopolitical landscape for generations to come.

APPENDIX

Additional Information on Military Leaders, Influential Battles, and Further Reading Suggestions

Military Leaders

1. **Alexander the Great:** King of Macedon and one of the most successful military commanders in history, Alexander the Great created an empire that spanned from Greece to Egypt and into present-day Pakistan.
2. **Julius Caesar:** Famous for his military exploits during the Gallic Wars, Julius Caesar was a Roman general and statesman who played a pivotal role in the transformation of the Roman Republic into the Roman Empire.
3. **William the Conqueror:** Norman duke who led the successful Norman invasion of England in 1066, forever changing the course of English history.
4. **Genghis Khan:** Founder of the Mongol Empire, Genghis Khan was a fierce warrior who successfully led his armies to conquer vast territories stretching from Europe to Asia.
5. **Napoleon Bonaparte:** French military leader who rose to prominence during the French Revolution and its associated wars, eventually becoming Emperor of France and leading his armies in numerous successful campaigns.

Influential Battles

1. **Battle of Marathon:** Fought in 490 BCE between Athens and Persia, this pivotal battle resulted in a surprise victory for Athens and marked a turning point in the Greco-Persian Wars.

2. **Battle of Hastings:** This decisive battle fought between William the Conqueror's Normans and King Harold II's Anglo-Saxons in 1066 ultimately determined England's future political landscape.
3. **Battle of Waterloo:** The climactic battle of 1815 that saw British Forces under the Duke of Wellington and Prussian forces under Field Marshal von Blücher decisively defeat Napoleon Bonaparte's army, ultimately leading to his exile and end of his reign as Emperor of France.
4. **D-Day (Battle of Normandy):** The largest seaborne invasion in history, which marked a turning point in World War II as Allied forces began the liberation of German-occupied Western Europe.
5. **Battle of Stalingrad:** Fought during World War II, this brutal and protracted battle between Soviet and German forces ultimately turned the tide against Nazi Germany on the Eastern Front.

Further Reading Suggestions

1. **The Art of War by Sun Tzu:** Perhaps the most famous treatise on military strategy, this ancient Chinese text has been studied and utilized by leaders worldwide for centuries.
2. **On War by Carl von Clausewitz:** A seminal work on military theory by this 19th-century Prussian general, it outlines the concepts of "absolute" and "real" war, as well as the all-important "fog of war."
3. **The Face of Battle by John Keegan:** This groundbreaking book looks at three historical battles (Agincourt, Waterloo, and the Somme) to offer a more comprehensive understanding of warfare from the perspective of those who fought in them.
4. **A History of Warfare by John Keegan:** Taking an anthropological approach to military history, this book explores various warriors from across human civilization, examining how societies engage in armed conflict.
5. **The Guns of August by Barbara Tuchman:** Focusing on the events leading up to World War I and its early days, this Pulitzer

Prize-winning account offers a detailed analysis of both political oversight and military strategy during this transformative period in history.

Glossary of Terms and Concepts

1. **Amphibious warfare:** Military operations involving the use of naval and land forces, typically in order to establish a beachhead or secure a coastal objective.
2. **Archer**: A soldier trained in the use of the bow and arrow as their primary weapon.
3. **Armada:** A large fleet of warships, particularly one assembled for naval warfare or strategic purposes.
4. **Armor:** Protective equipment worn by soldiers to defend against enemy attacks, including plate armor, chainmail, and shields.
5. **Artillery:** Large-caliber guns used to fire heavy projectiles over long distances, often employed in support of infantry and cavalry units.
6. **Barracks:** Permanent buildings or other accommodations designed for housing military personnel.
7. **Battlefield:** The location where opposing forces engage in combat. A battlefield may encompass land, air, and/or sea dimensions.
8. **Blitzkrieg:** A German term meaning "lightning war," this tactic involved rapid, violent attacks intended to quickly overwhelm enemy defenses.
9. **Blockade:** The use of naval forces to prevent ships from entering or exiting a specific area, usually to disrupt commerce or transport routes for strategic purposes.
10. **Border conflict:** A clash between two neighboring states over territorial disputes or other issues related to their shared border.
11. **Bunker:** A fortified underground structure designed to protect personnel and materials from hostile actions such as bombardment or invasion.

12. **Calvary:** Mounted soldiers trained in swordsmanship, archery, and/or the use of lances; typically used as scouts, skirmishers, or shock troops in battle.
13. **Campaign:** A series of military operations carried out with a specific objective or goal during wartime.
14. **Cannon fodder:** An informal term for soldiers regarded as expendable and used primarily to absorb enemy fire during battles or assaults.
15. **Catapult:** An ancient engine of war, consisting of a wheeled frame with an arm that launched projectiles such as stones or incendiary devices.
16. **Citadel:** A fortress or fortified structure built to protect a town or city from enemy threats.
17. **Coastal defense**: Military measures taken to protect coastlines and harbors from enemy attacks, including the deployment of naval vessels and artillery installations.
18. **Command structure:** The hierarchy of authority within a military organization, which typically includes commanders, staff officers, and enlisted personnel.
19. **Counterinsurgency:** Military and political efforts aimed at countering the activities of insurgent groups or other non-state actors within a specific territory.
20. **Coup d'état:** A sudden and often violent seizure of power by a small group within a government or military organization, typically carried out by overthrowing established leaders.
21. **Defeat in detail:** The tactic of defeating an enemy force by intentionally waiting for it to separate into smaller groups before launching a concentrated attack on each in succession.
22. **Espionage:** The practice of secretly obtaining information about an enemy's plans, actions, or capabilities using spies or other covert means.
23. **Field Marshal:** The highest-ranking military officer in some countries, responsible for overall command and direction of armed forces during times of war.

24. **Fortification:** Defensive structures and works constructed to protect against enemy attacks, including walls, ditches, towers, and bunkers.

25. **Guerrilla warfare:** Irregular military actions carried out by small bands of fighters using tactics such as ambushes and raids to harass or undermine an opposing force's capabilities.

26. **Infantry:** Soldiers who fight on foot, typically armed with rifles, pistols, grenades, and other portable weapons; infantry units are the mainstay of ground warfare.

27. **Logistics:** The planning and management of resources required to support military operations, such as transportation, food, supplies, equipment maintenance and repair, and medical care.

28. **Machine gun:** A rapidly firing, automatic firearm capable of shooting many bullets in a short period of time, often used for suppressing enemy positions or providing covering fire for advancing troops.

29. **Mercenary:** A professional soldier hired by a foreign government or other entity to fight in armed conflicts, often for personal gain or profit.

30. **Militia:** An irregular force of citizen soldiers, typically organized on a local level and used to supplement regular military forces in times of crisis or emergency.

31. **Naval warfare:** Combat involving the use of warships, submarines, and other naval forces, typically carried out on or under the surface of the ocean, in seas, and in coastal waters.

32. **Occupation:** The act of a military force seizing control of a foreign territory and exercising authority over its population for a period.

33. **Paratrooper:** A soldier trained in parachuting from aircraft and performing airborne assaults or other military operations.

34. **Partisan:** A member of an irregular military force that fights against an occupying power, typically using guerrilla warfare tactics to resist enemy control.

35. **Reconnaissance:** Military activities aimed at gathering information about an enemy's composition, capabilities,

movements, or intentions, usually conducted by scouts, aerial surveillance, or other specialized units.

36. **Siege:** The prolonged surrounding and blockading of a fortified place or city by an opposing force in an attempt to force its surrender.

37. **Sniper: A** highly skilled sharpshooter trained in long-range marksmanship, typically tasked with eliminating high-priority targets or providing cover for friendly forces from concealed positions.

38. **Special forces:** Elite military units specially trained and equipped to conduct unconventional warfare or covert operations behind enemy lines.

39. **Strategy:** The art and science of planning and directing military activities to achieve specific goals or objectives in conflict situations.

40. **Tactics:** The methods used by commanders and their forces to achieve success on the battlefield through the deployment of troops, weapons, and other resources.

41. **Tank:** An armored fighting vehicle designed primarily for engaging enemy forces with direct fire weaponry and providing protected mobility to its crew.

42. **Trench warfare:** A style of combat characterized by opposing forces occupying parallel networks of fortified trenches while attempting to attack the enemy's positions with artillery fire or infantry assaults.

43. **War dog:** Canines utilized in various roles throughout history, including tracking, guarding, carrying messages, detecting mines and explosives, as well as search and rescue operations.

44. **Warlord:** A leader who exercises military control over a region in the absence of central authority or because of political strife; warlords often maintain their power through force or alliances with other armed groups.

45. **Weapons of mass destruction (WMD):** Weapons that can cause widespread death, injuries, or damage to the environment

and infrastructure, including nuclear, biological, and chemical weaponry.

46. **Zulu warrior:** A member of the South African Zulu tribe known for their exceptional fighting skills and tactics throughout history, particularly during the Anglo-Zulu War of 1879.

Made in the USA
Columbia, SC
19 December 2024

50094129R00061